Living With Jos Buttler

Six Weeks in English Cricket's Summer of Love

Published by Green Publications

Copyright © 2019 Adam Tangent

Adam Tangent has asserted his right
under the Copyright, Designs and Patents Act 1988
to be identified as the author of this work.

ISBN 978-1-84396-571-8

A catalogue record for
this book is available from the British Library
and the American Library of Congress

No part of this book may be
copied or reproduced in any way or form
without the prior written consent
of the publisher

Cover design and artwork
Paul Morris
www.mostlygreenstuff.com

Typesetting and pre-press production
eBook Versions
27 Old Gloucester Street
London WC1N 3AX
www.ebookversions.com

For my son and his sister MOP

Living With Jos Buttler

Six Weeks in English Cricket's Summer of Love

Adam Tangent

GREEN PUBLISHING

Stanhope:

Yes, I am his hero.

Osbourne:

It's quite natural.

Stanhope:

You think so?

Osbourne:

Small boys at school generally have their heroes.

Stanhope:

Yes. Small boys at school do.

(Taken from *Journey's End* by R.C. Sherriff)

August 2019

For the past few weeks I have been troubled by a recurring thought or image, and it has also come to me in my sleep as a full-blown dream, in which the final act of the Cricket World Cup Final departs from what actually happened. This always involves the last ball of the super over. Not the delivery itself but Jason Roy fielding the ball in the outfield, the return to Jos Buttler the wicket-keeper, and the demolition of the stumps for the match winning run out.

I have found myself fretting about each part of this sequence. What if Roy had fumbled the ball in the deep, as he had earlier in the over? But more persistent has been the thought of Buttler messing up. He might have dropped Roy's throw, but more troubling is what he does next with his hands. After catching the ball in both hands, they part so that he can stretch with the ball in hand to break the wickets – but the worrying possibility occurs to me now of his hitting the stumps with the wrong hand, or spilling the ball before he can get to the stumps. Two days ago, in the third Ashes test at Headingley, the Australian spinner Nathan Lyon had a much easier job to run out England's spinner Jack Leach to win the match but dropped a gentle return. In modern cricket-speak, Buttler trusted his skills, completed the run out and England squeaked home to World Cup glory.

Half an hour earlier, my son, with whom I watched the final on TV, had gone down on his knees to offer up a prayer to any deity who might have a care about the fortunes of the English cricket team. As an atheist, or at best an agnostic, I suggested he might as well pray to our cat, Rupert, but, despite his own godlessness, he went ahead and said a prayer in earnest. I don't know how this was phrased but it may well have run along these lines: 'Dear God in heaven, I will believe if you could only do this one thing – please, please let Jos Buttler be on the winning side.'

What Osbourne says in *Journey's End* about small boys and hero worship is all very well, but sometimes it is necessary to remind my son that there are ten other players in a cricket team. This usually falls on deaf ears, and his personal attachment to Jos Buttler is such that had any of those alternative storylines come into play, the personal anguish doesn't bear thinking about. They didn't, but they could have, which remains a worrying thought, and partly explains why the World Cup Final was such an exhausting emotional experience for people who cared about the result and the players involved.

When it was over a rest period was required for all concerned, probably rather more than the two weeks the ECB allowed before the start of the Ashes. Buttler and Stokes, the heroes of England's run chase and the super over, missed the Ireland test match, whereas Bairstow played and batted like a man in shock and bagged a pair.

But now the Ashes has started, which means that in our house Buttler-watch has started up all over again.

Third Test: Headingley

22-26 August

Thursday 22 August 2019

It's GCSE results day. This may inconvenience my fourteen-year-old son in a couple of years' time, but for now his priority is the third test against Australia at Headingley. Unfortunately for him we are on holiday in Devon, without access to Sky Sports. However, he seems determined not to let the family holiday get in the way of what really matters and greets me this morning with, 'Bancroft might be dropped', before placing an order for two pieces of toast with strawberry jam.

And then, 'Can we not go anywhere. I want to listen to TMS.' (Test Match Special) We have brought a digital radio with us and the chalet also has a TV for the evening highlights on Channel 5. He also has his phone and announces that his 'new favourite hobby is listening to BBC Radio Somerset', presumably because it mentions his hero (Buttler is from Somerset) more than other media outlets. So far, his appreciation of Devon has been held in check by his conviction that everything in Somerset is far superior, despite never, to our knowledge, ever having been to Somerset. The outings earlier in the week, to Bigbury-on-Sea and Burgh Island, and the coastal path between South Sands (near Salcombe) and Bolt Head – both in perfect weather – seem to have counted for very little compared to the prospect of visiting Taunton and the county ground's museum.

These outings were conducted without the distraction of a test match happening somewhere else in the country, but today promises to be more fraught. Having had the better of the second test at Lords, England are unchanged, except for an adjustment to the batting order – Buttler dropping from six to seven, below Jonny Bairstow the wicket-keeper. This isn't exactly a massive story but ensures that my son is even more grumpy for the drive across bits of Dartmoor and our exploration of Exeter in the afternoon. Despite a promising forecast, it is, of course, overcast in Leeds, and Joe Root has decided to bowl. There is much repetition on the car radio of the old cricketing / Headingley adage that you 'look up, not down at t' pitch' before deciding whether to bat or bowl. Along with a lengthy rain delay, this means that England, and more particularly their new number seven Jos Buttler, shouldn't be batting today, which makes the day a bit easier for my son to bear.

The drive to Devon last Sunday had coincided with Stokes and Buttler batting England to safety during the morning session of the final day of the Lords test. I had suggested we ignore the cricket until lunch and listen to music instead. This way he could spare himself the agony and suspense; and if, by lunch, Buttler had established himself and got into the forties, he could listen in the afternoon in a more relaxed state. (I had employed this tactic in 2009 on the last day of the Lords test when we still had to take five Australian wickets. I was taking the car to be serviced and had to wait around in Walthamstow for a couple of hours. Only when I was on the way back on the North Circular did I allow myself to tune in to TMS, to find that Flintoff had polished off Australia in quick time, and that I'd missed one of the great spells of fast bowling.)

Last Sunday Buttler had only got to 31 by lunch – nine short of the comforting respectability of forty – and was out straight after without adding to his score, perversely just as the M5 entered Somerset.

* * *

The delays for rain and bad light in Leeds, still don't make Exeter Cathedral a more attractive proposition for either of my children, and we are also put-off by the £7.50 charged for entrance. Instead we split up – mother and daughter going one way, while I accompany my son to WHSmith in search of the latest edition of *Wisden Cricket Monthly*, which features an Anatomy of a Genius – Jos Buttler Exclusive interview.

Friday 23 August

Today has been an unmitigated disaster. Buttler's score of 5 is about par in England's total of 67. Michael Vaughan provided absolution on the radio with his comment that you couldn't really blame Buttler for throwing the bat with England seven wickets down, but this only feeds my son's sense of grievance at his demotion below Bairstow in the batting order.

The day had dawned very promisingly, in Leeds and in Devon. Having admitted on Thursday to excursion burn-out after just five days, my wife took me up on my suggestion that we cut short our stay by one day. The original proposal had involved stopping in Taunton, but this is forgotten in my children's enthusiasm for going home.

By the time we've packed and returned the keys of the holiday home, England are already three down, and as we are turning out of the farm / campsite Stokes swishes at a full wide ball and is caught behind. 34-4. At this point father and son forget their issue with the batting order and are happy that it's Bairstow who is going out to face the music / Josh Hazelwood.

The downside of travelling back today, apart from England's batting, is that it is the Friday before the August Bank Holiday, and one for which there is an unusually good forecast. Almost as soon as we get onto the M5 it becomes clear that we have company. Jonathan Agnew makes several references on TMS to families stuck in Bank Holiday traffic being made more miserable by the clatter of wickets, which doesn't help.

When Joe Denly perishes (he's England's top scorer with 12), Buttler is in with about twenty minutes to go until lunch. I don't repeat my suggestion of switching the radio off and trying again in an hour or so with the hope of hearing better news. This has to be endured. Bairstow doesn't last long but for a horrible moment we aren't sure who is out. 'He's nicked it,' isn't very helpful on the radio.

As he had in the second innings at Lords, Buttler leaves the ball well outside his off stump, except for one trademark drive to the extra cover boundary. Woakes is on strike for the final over before lunch but provokes a groan from the back seat of the car by taking a single from the third ball of the over. But Buttler survives and we crawl towards Taunton with hope intact.

This has been extinguished by the time we stop at a crowded service station somewhere near Bristol. Woakes was out first ball after lunch, leaving Buttler – as my son had foretold – stranded with the tail. This time his trademark extra cover drive went straight to the fielder, Usman Khawaja. A foot either side and it would have been a boundary, but the fielder – as at Lords in the second innings – doesn't have to move.

The only consolation as England toil in the field in the afternoon is that we're not driving towards Devon and Cornwall. We at least are moving. And for my son, there is the consolation, waiting for him at home, of his new cricket cap, for which he has received a delivery notification. It turns out to be bright green and slightly too big (and has something about it akin to a deerstalker) but he is delighted with it.

Sunday 25 August

Another long day yesterday on the sofa for my son, watching the cricket in his new – and he has decided lucky – cap. In terms of England's tentative fightback that remains to be seen.

A friend who was going to Headingley yesterday texted after England's collapse on Friday to say he didn't want to go anymore. I reminded him of our day at Headingley in 2001 watching Mark Butcher's 173. That day had begun with the certain expectation of comprehensive defeat. For the first half hour Atherton and Trescothick had groped around in gloomy light and then got out. To make matters worse we had been forced to leave behind a bottle of Rioja we'd brought along for lunch. With typical Yorkshire generosity the ground regulations prohibited bottles of wine, and I'd had to hide it in a hedge in somebody's front garden and retrieve it at the end of the day.

But later, when the sun came out, Butcher had played the innings of his life. Unlike some of the England batsmen in this test match, his footwork and defence had been immaculate. Jason Roy, on the other hand, fell over after lunch yesterday trying to play a forward defensive shot to a good ball from Pat Cummins, and was bowled, and provoked a snort of 'Bambi on ice' from Botham, who was on commentary.

Better footwork from Denly and Root, and my son's lucky cap, stopped the rot later in the day, and a stand of over a hundred now means that England supporters have the alarming sensation of hope before the start of play on day four.

It was something of a relief today when my son left his place at the end of the sofa and went off at lunchtime to play for the

Sunday men's team at his cricket club. The post-lunch slump was easier to bear in solitude – specifically Buttler being run out for one – but by the time Stokes had got it down to about thirty needed, I made my wife come downstairs and watch the closing moments with me.

Meanwhile my son was fielding on a village green somewhere, piecing together bits of the action from Headingley via the shouts from the clubhouse, which had a TV. Later when his side were batting, he took to social media – the family WhatsApp group – to fight Buttler's corner. When his grandmother posted, 'What a warrior Stokes is!' he texted back with, 'Owed me! Sold Jos down the river…So annoying! Called Jos through and then sent him back.'

With Stokes in the doghouse over the run out, his good news story is the contribution of England's number eleven, Jack Leach – one run in the last wicket stand of 76. Leach has the added advantage of having been Jos Buttler's best man and they are old friends according to my son. Leach's main contribution to the unbearable tension of the final overs were the delays whilst he cleaned his glasses after every couple of balls, which were misting up in the heat of battle. It seemed somehow fitting that his one run should have been taken from the relentless Pat Cummins – a fidgety nudge off his hip from a bowler who looks like an American football star, all wide shoulders and perfect teeth.

Monday 26 August

The bank holiday is also a much-needed day off from the Ashes. A couple of weeks ago, as we were leaving the abandoned first day of the Lords test match in pouring rain, and with my son in tears at his misfortune, I promised him that we could go to day five at Headingley if the match went that far. But it hasn't. Day one of the Lords test was his only chance to see live international cricket this summer but seemed doomed well before we emerged from St John's Wood tube station to persistent drizzle. He had spent the week leading up to it comparing weather forecasts and quoting me percentage precipitation predictions, and trying to avoid the Met Office figure of 90% for each hour of play. Even when it stopped raining, briefly, during what should have been the lunch interval, water was still falling from the stand above us, spilling, as if from a spurting gargoyle, from the guttering beneath the Compton Stand Upper Tier. One of our group had prepared a summery picnic, which included cubes of chilled watermelon and stuffed vine leaves, but found no takers.

To make matters worse I had a ticket to go with a friend on day two – of course a dry day with pleasant sunshine. By the start of play my son had come to terms with this and rang me to wish me a good day, but it hadn't been without a struggle. When two visits to the Lords ticket office (in the rain on day one) yielded nothing, he took to the internet / dark web and presented me with a number of expensive options. I ended up speaking to one dodgy character on the phone, who wanted £250 for a child ticket in the gloom / wind tunnel that is the Lower Tier of the Compton & Edrich Stand. These alternative suppliers also required payment up front, which didn't seem to faze him but persuaded his parents to give up.

I had gone early on day two, still half pondering whether to approach one of the ticket touts who line the pavement from St John's Wood station to the ground – 'Anyone looking for tickets for the match. Anyone selling…I'll buy tickets…' – so that I could then ring home like a fairy godmother with the news, 'Get on the train, you are going to the ball'. In the end I avoided them all together and went down a parallel side street to the shops in St John's Wood to buy my lunch in the Tesco Metro.

It was nice to see some cricket, but there was nothing especially memorable, or a Buttler cameo for my son to resent missing out on. In many respects the cricket was rather predictable: Roy was out for 0, caught behind to Hazelwood; Root was LBW to Hazelwood, falling across his stumps; Denly was hit by a bouncer; and England again failed to get anywhere near 400 in their first innings. And then when Australia batted Warner fell cheaply to Broad. Not a great day of test cricket, and it had none of the drama of day four when Archer roughed-up Smith, or the last day when England came close to winning. On the way out, at the end of the day's play, my friend and I gave in to temptation and each collected a pile of other people's plastic beer glasses and then, ignoring the fact that we have both turned fifty, visited the 'redemption point' for a small pay out.

My wife had been tempted to pay over the odds to get him a ticket, but previous experience of chasing around the country hoping to see Jos Buttler bat had persuaded me that it was better, on this occasion, to stop digging. This has included an overnight stay in Bristol to watch an ODI against the West Indies in which Buttler made 2. The cricketing headlines for everyone else were quick runs from Moen Ali and Chris Gayle, but that was soon eclipsed by the Ben Stokes punch up, which took place later that night.

And then following Buttler's maiden test century against India last summer, my son got wind that he'd be playing for Lancashire a few days later in a 20/20 match against Kent at Canterbury. This didn't require a hotel room because his grandparents live nearly opposite the county ground, but again didn't go entirely to plan. On this occasion Buttler was out first ball to the part-time leg spinner Joe Denly. This was quickly explained away as the inevitable consequence of his exertions in the test match and put to one side as he concentrated on a more tangible result – a selfie with the great man, taken on the boundary before the match started. As soon as Buttler came out for the fielding drills and warm-up he was nabbed by Sky for an interview about his hundred at Trent Bridge. Throughout the interview my son loitered at the boundary edge about thirty yards away, hoping to be noticed / get an autograph. When he was named one of the Five Cricketers of the Year in 2019, *Wisden* noted Buttler's tendency 'to see others' point of view', and on this occasion that included a thirteen-year-old boy watching on anxiously in the background. I had assumed that my son would continue there unnoticed, but as soon as the interview was over, Butter went to talk to him and pose for the obligatory selfie.

Obviously, the pressure of meeting your hero is considerable. What do you say and how do you go about looking natural in a photograph? My son would later disown his own facial expression in the picture, but it remains a treasured Buttler artefact.

This problem – looking your best in a selfie – didn't arise in the second half of the 1970s. Collecting autographs was an anonymous and largely silent transaction. If you were feeling really ambitious you could write to Jim'll Fix It and request to meet one of your heroes, but generally speaking you kept your distance. Thankfully, Jimmy Savile didn't fix it for me to bowl at Geoff Boycott, so I had to make do with his autograph. The 'autograph' is now starting to look a bit old school and young cricket fans, like my son, don't always seem to know what they are doing. This was evident when I witnessed him getting Kane Williamson's autograph at Lords. This was under the media centre as Williamson returned from a net session at the Nursery End, still wearing his pads and helmet. My son thrust out his autograph book for Williamson to sign and then looked at the signature and said, 'Who are you?'

'Kane Williamson!' was the straight-batted, if slightly indignant reply.

If my son's attachment to Jos Buttler has sometimes felt like a love affair, sadly it has also often felt like a doomed one. The only England v Australia match he's seen so far was an ODI on a gloomy day at Lords in September 2015, with Buttler horribly out of form following a run of low scores in the test series, and about to be replaced for the rest of the series by Bairstow. Buttler's brief stay at the wicket – he was LBW to Maxwell for 0 – hardly registered with the rest of the crowd, who were too busy booing the Australians and the umpires, following Stokes' dismissal for 'obstructing the field'. From the Compton Upper Tier, it looked as if Starc had hurled the ball back to the wicket keeper as someone might rev their engine in traffic. It had hall. I was then thirty-seven years old and a member of staff, and ended up having to go to a chiropractor for several months and at considerable expense because of the shock to my back. Now the dog thrower allows me to bowl at a lively pace and come down from a height not unlike Joel Garner.

In the absence of any significant contribution from Buttler in the Headingley test, my son fills the void with the next best thing – Buttler's friend, Jack Leach. I now know that he did a physics degree and that his favourite drink is Thatcher's cider with bits of chopped strawberry – a concoction my son makes in the afternoon with his last can of Thatcher's Rose Cider. (Unwisely I caved into his Thatcher's cider campaign and bought him four cans of the sweetest cider they do.)

He also shows me a picture on his phone of Leach and other members of the England team re-creating his single (the run that levelled the scores) out in the middle at an empty, still sun-drenched Headingley.

There is one nod to the real hero of Headingley, when he claims to be 'feeling his glute', something I imagine he picked up from the post-match interviews with Stokes.

I am not sure exactly when my son swore his oath of allegiance to Jos Buttler. (At home he presumes first name terms and it's just 'Jos' this and 'Jos' that. Not an option for his father unless I want to sound like a tennis commentator.) I think it came sometime after his test debut against India in July 2014, and the winter tour to the West Indies, which is a shame as Buttler's form was excellent in this period. Unfortunately, the hero worship probably got into full swing around the time that

Buttler was dropped as England's test wicket-keeper batsman, after a poor run of scores in the 2015 Ashes and then against Pakistan in the UAE. The dastardly figure of Jonny Bairstow then took the gloves and grabbed the opportunity with lots of runs against South Africa, and that was that for a bit.

Buttler mania may not have been quite what it was to become later, at the end of May 2014, but the fact that his father was going to an ODI against Sri Lanka at Lords without him, still went down very badly with my then ten-year old son. Sangakkara made a predictable and typically efficient hundred and Sri Lanka set England 301 to win. This would now be regarded as a routine chase, but on this occasion England's top four included the not so explosive batting of Alistair Cook and Gary Ballance. Buttler came in with England five wickets down, and with apparently no chance of winning. There was no obvious star quality in the way he walked to the middle. No breezy Botham-style swinging of the arms or jaunty chewing like Viv Richards, but instead, the hint of a trudge / plod to the crease. But the crouch over the bat and the explosive hitting recalled what I'd read as a boy about Gilbert Jessop in Christopher Martin-Jenkins' *The Complete Who's Who of Test Cricketers* – 'The most famous hitter in cricket history…he was consistent as well as pulverising' - and the picture of Jessop ('The Croucher') bent low over his bat. Almost immediately the momentum of the game shifted and the atmosphere in the ground perked up. Ravi Bopara, who had previously looked half asleep, suddenly seemed to wake up and started running quick singles. Buttler made 121 from seventy-four balls, but fell to Malinga with England just short of victory – not from an in-swinging Yorker, most of which had disappeared to the extra-cover boundary, but run out, attempting another cheeky single.

It has also been a matter of some regret and recrimination that I was there at the Rose Bowl for Buttler's first test innings, whilst my son was visiting his cousins. Had Buttler-watch been fully operational at that time, I doubt he'd have ever forgiven my treachery in going to the test match in secret. Eventually I gave myself away by recounting the day's play in too much detail. At one point towards the end of play, Anderson was swinging the ball so prodigiously that he experimented bowling round the wicket to right handers. I had moved to a position behind the bowler's arm to watch what he was doing, but later gave such a full account of Anderson's spell that my son smelt a rat and I had to make a full confession.

After a rather careless defeat in the second test at Lords, the Rose Bowl match was very easy viewing for an England supporter. Bell and Cook scored heavily against ordinary Indian bowling and Buttler thrashed a rapid 85 after lunch – which, unfortunately, is 83 more runs than my son has seen him make in the flesh in the four matches (two test matches, an ODI and 20/20 Blast) he's attended so far in pursuit of his hero.

The unfairness of life is also apparent to my son in the circumstances surrounding Buttler's spell in the wilderness, after being dropped for the final test against Pakistan in the UAE in November 2015. Buttler hadn't been alone in struggling to bat against Pakistan's spinners on turning pitches but was the one dropped and so unable to enjoy the friendlier surfaces in South Africa, England's next stop. In January in Cape Town England scored 629 in their first innings (Stokes 258 and Bairstow 150 not out) and South Africa replied with 627.

* * *

Commentaries on contemporary British society might be expected to separate life before the Brexit referendum from life after it. My son's view of recent history is rather different and would identify two distinct periods – before Buttler's test recall in May 2018, and after it. He knows exactly where he was when he heard the good news, that Buttler had been picked for the first test of the summer against Pakistan at Lords – Art, period four just before lunch, from where he covertly texted me this measured response: 'Jos back in the England test squad!!!!! What t f???? YESS!'

But this happy day was more than two years away at the start of 2016. It could hardly be described as two years in the wilderness because for all of that period Buttler was one of England's most successful white ball cricketers, was vice-captain of the England ODI team, and successfully captained the side in the series in Bangladesh, in Eoin Morgan's absence. But his omission from the test side was a private grief for my son, and a great injustice – 'He's way better than' so and so… etc, etc. And as much as he celebrated Buttler's success in white ball cricket, it also constituted a dangerous catch-22 – perhaps confirming in the eyes of commentators and selectors that he was just a one day specialist, and keeping him so busy in various short forms of the game that he never had the chance to change this perception by playing any first class cricket. The record breaking forty-six ball hundred against Pakistan in November 2015, following the disastrous test series (England lost 2-0 and Buttler was dropped after the second test) was, therefore, a bitter-sweet experience for his most loyal follower. Another white ball hundred against South Africa in Bloemfontein followed in February, but it rankled with my son that it was

Bairstow, not Buttler, enhancing his average on some friendly batting surfaces in the test series against South Africa.

Why could Buttler bat with such skill and assurance in the World T20 that followed in March and April but have sometimes looked such an uncertain starter against the red ball? Possibly because he hardly ever played against a red ball. His one County Championship appearance in 2016 was against Middlesex in September – his first Championship game since 2014. He scored 16 in the first innings batting at number six, but then opened in the second innings when Lancashire, who had been set 309 to win from 44 overs, required a one-day innings. He hit three fours and a six in the first eight deliveries he faced but was then dismissed by Steve Finn for 26.

The bitter-sweet theme continued that winter for the England tour of Bangladesh and India. Buttler may have lost his place as first choice wicket-keeper batsman, but he was at least still in the squad. Bairstow didn't break a finger or tear a hamstring, as my son had hoped, but Buttler did get his chance – as a batting replacement for Gary Ballance and Ben Duckett in the third test against India at Mohali. Substituting for two of the ugliest batsmen (technically and aesthetically) to have ever played for England wasn't exactly the glorious return my son had planned for him. Between them they had managed 116 runs in eight innings against Bangladesh. Ballance was then dropped (again) for the India series, but Duckett staggered on with scores of 13, 5 and 0, whilst my son, back in England, raged at the folly of James Whitaker, the Chairman of Selectors. Finally, when he was the last cab on the rank, Buttler was brought back for the third test as a specialist batsman, and did well in the rest of the series against a dangerous spin attack with scores of 43, 18, 76, 6 not out, 5 and 6 not out. An average of 38.5. However many times my son added them up and divided them, the average remained stubbornly just short of the magic forty. But surely, he reasoned, enough for Buttler to be retained for the home tests in 2017 against South Africa and the West Indies.

Instead, 2017 would prove to be his low point on Buttler-watch. Not only did the selectors not stick with Buttler for the first test of the summer against South Africa, they added insult to injury by bringing back Gary Ballance, and also a Gary Ballance clone, the robotic opener Keaton Jennings. Neither moved their feet, or their arms, or scored any runs, and both had been dropped by the second series of the summer against the West Indies. For some reason, Buttler's sensible batting against India in the winter counted for nothing. When Ballance was dropped, he was replaced by the Essex batsman Tom Westley.

At the end of the first week of August in 2017, we drove back from our holiday in Brittany accompanied by commentary of Lancashire's county championship game against Hampshire. Desperate for Buttler to score some runs and press his claim for the Ashes squad, my son grew more and more disgruntled with the young opener Hameed for his selfishly long stay at the crease. When Buttler eventually got a bat, he was dismissed for the second time in the match by Fidel Edwards for 21. Not what the doctor ordered.

Even in the ODI series that followed the test series, events conspired against Buttler. He only batted twice in the five-match series. At the Oval, in the fourth match, he scored a crucial 43 not out in a match winning partnership with Moeen Ali; but we had opted to travel to Bristol for the third match, in which he lasted four balls and scored 2. To make matters worse, Bairstow scored two centuries opening the batting.

But the real villain was James Whitaker, who signed off as chairman of selectors by leaving Buttler out of the touring party to Australia. In what looked to my son like a deliberate provocation / piss-take, Gary Ballance was selected – presumably not to strike fear into the hearts of the Australians or score any runs, but on the grounds that he'd once shared a house with Joe Root. The ESPN Cricket Info website described it as 'an apology of a squad – a deeply uninspiring blend of the tried, tested and discarded brought back to the boil with a sprinkling of fresh ingredients like the manky carcass of an ancient Sunday roast.'

Wednesday 28 August

On the day that Boris Johnson announced his plan to prorogue Parliament, my son's contribution to the no deal debate comes from a fairly obscure, but in some ways rather predictable source. From the back of the car he reads out a response to an article in the *Somerset Gazette* tweeted by Jos Buttler's sister, highlighting the likely shortage of key medicines in the event of no deal.

We are on our way back from a local wildlife park. With the fourth test at Old Trafford not starting until next Wednesday – his first day back at school – my son has begun casting around for other sources of amusement. Yesterday he watched several episodes from series four of *Poldark*, and he has also threatened to start watching the entire series of *Peaky Blinders* on BBC I player. Mindful of the need to get him and his sister out of the house, without it involving a visit to the nets, I agreed to take them to Paradise Wildlife Park. Even more of it has been turned into play areas since we were last there, and as they're too old for diggers and Thomas the Tank Engine, and are only interested in seeing the big cats – all of whom are asleep apart from one Jaguar – it ends up being a very short visit.

I have refused to buy any more Thatcher's cider, so my son has retaliated by making apple juice. Having initially refused to help I end up peeling most of the apples but have now left him to it.

Thursday 29 August

This afternoon my son showed me a picture which he says shows Buttler on holiday in Monaco. In the background there is a small jetty and some boats. The buildings do look like they could be in the south of France, but could also be anywhere on the Mediterranean. His other evidence for his Monaco theory is that his hero is wearing 'French-style shorts', whatever they are.

Other forensic discussion of the picture centres on the glass he is holding – a pint glass which says Gaymers, a make of cider. To forestall any more talk of buying him cider, I decide that now is the time to mention newspaper reports I've read in the last couple of days that have suggested Buttler might be dropped, or 'rested', for the next test at Old Trafford. Either Buttler or Jason Roy might make way for the young Surrey batsman Ollie Pope. This might explain why he's left the country, I add. My son is indignant at the muddled thinking which has lumped Buttler and Roy together in the debate over selection and argues vehemently that Buttler's last three dismissals can be put down to bad luck – obviously the run out in the second innings at Leeds, but also the way two well-timed attacking shots have gone straight to the fielder. (I resist the temptation to play devil's advocate and counter that this, it could be argued, makes them bad shots, and instead nod in agreement.) Whereas Roy, he continues, has looked like a walking wicket on a par with Keaton Jennings. Fair point.

But what if he is exhausted after the World Cup, as has been widely reported?

'No, they won't drop him. He's one of the leaders in the

dressing room.' And then becoming more sanguine, 'And if they do, he'll definitely be back for South Africa.'

Because Buttler missed out on the last test series in South Africa, the one where Stokes and Bairstow scored big hundreds in Cape Town, he's convinced that South Africa represents a sure-fire opportunity for Buttler to fill his boots and boost his average, which he has been monitoring nervously as it has slipped below thirty-five.

Friday 30 August

Two things were cleared up today. First of all, Buttler's holiday destination was in fact Menorca not Monaco. The picture he'd shown me yesterday was taken, he now thinks, in Citadella, the old capital – around which we had dragged him and his equally grumpy and unenthusiastic sister only just over three weeks ago. Suddenly it doesn't seem such a boring place to visit.

And at lunchtime the squad for Old Trafford was announced. Earlier my son had tried to fortify his doubting father by quoting the views of four of *The Times*' journalists, who all had Buttler in their team for the next test. They and he prove to be correct. Buttler and Roy are in the squad.

The bad / sad news is that Anderson won't be. Long before Jos Buttler came along, my son's original cricketing idol had been James Anderson. Like Anderson, he had also begun bowling without looking where he was bowling to, but that was probably the only similarity. He certainly didn't possess what might be called a repeatable action. A 'frog in a washing machine' was how one sympathetic coach described it. Soon after that he decided to concentrate on his batting. He can do the Buttler hockey slap through square cover, and has even incorporated the shoulder twitch just before the bowler releases. At some point last year, the words 'Fuck it' mysteriously also became etched on the top of his bat handle, as had been captured by an eagle-eyed photographer when Buttler's bat was lying on the ground. *Wisden* described it as the 'most significant expletive since Mike Gatting addressed Shakoor Rana in 1987', and my son has certainly taken it to heart. This season he also paid someone at his cricket club to remove the stickers on his bat and sand it down – I suspect so that he can get new stickers which match whatever bat Buttler is using. All of which is much easier than bowling six balls in the same place.

He still has great faith in Anderson's powers of recovery, even at thirty-seven. When I suggest that'll be it for England's greatest bowler, he bats it away. 'No, he's definitely going to South Africa.'

Later, when I am in the kitchen cooking his tea, I am summoned to the living room by a shout of excitement: 'Leachy's in the pod!' He's watching the 20/20 Blast game from Taunton between Somerset and Middlesex. England's spinner and number 11 batsman is doing an interview before the game about his innings of 1 not out in the Headingley test. This match also features Tom Banton, a very stylish attacking batsmen, who my son has started to follow with keen interest – a sort of baby Buttler in the making. He's now made it on to what my son calls his 'podium', along with Buttler and Leach. Banton gets runs and Somerset post a huge total, but then bowl terribly and Middlesex knock off the runs with time to spare.

Sunday 1 September

The latest holiday snap from Menorca to reach my son's phone via social media shows Buttler and his wife smartly dressed, on their way, he says, to a wedding. Back in 2017, when the selectors left him out of the squad to tour Australia, Buttler's own wedding / honeymoon photos were all my son was left with as the nights drew in and winter took hold. Suddenly he started extoling the attractions of a very expensive part of the Italian coast, and suggesting it as the destination for our next holiday, forgetting that his dad is a school teacher, not an IPL superstar.

Following the honeymoon, my son kept tabs on Buttler's performances in the relative obscurity of the Bangladesh Premier League, and then on to the Sydney Thunders in the Australian Big Bash.

This period tested my son's mettle, but Buttler's star continued to shine just as brightly in his private universe. There is definitely something to be said for a more exclusive arrangement with your hero. When I was in Year 9, or rather the third year, Ian Botham was performing miracles against the Australians in the summer of 1981, but at no point did I feel the need to follow his fortunes closely. It would have been like telling everyone that your favourite band were The Beatles. And Botham enjoyed plenty of good fortune and success without me taking special interest. Instead I selected a succession of cricketing heroes – all batsmen – based purely on liking the sound of their names: first there was Brian Luckhurst, at the awakening of my cricketing consciousness in the early seventies, and then two overseas players, Gordon Greenidge and Sadiq

Mohammad. Sadiq – the youngest of the famous Mohammad brothers, who all played for Pakistan – was a particular obsession at the end of the 1970s, but for no obvious reason I can account for looking back now. Quite why I should have been drawn to a diminutive left-handed opener with a pirate moustache and a distinctive twiddle of his bat, I have no idea. By comparison, Buttler with his rare talent and debonair looks, is an obvious choice. And compared to following the fortunes of a Pakistani opening batsman in the miserable summer of 1978, against Willis, Hendrick and Botham in his prime, supporting someone as successful as Buttler seems like a walk in the park. In the third and final test against Pakistan in 1978, I recall being desperate for Sadiq to haul his series average upwards towards respectability, after two failures at Lords in the second test. Conditions, as is generally the case at Headingley, were not ideal. It wasn't one of the great test matches, and there was, as they say, a lot of weather about. So much so that Pakistan's first innings was spread across five days - the first four days of the match, plus the rest day on Sunday. For several days I kept up a lonely vigil, willing his survival between the rain breaks as he inched his way towards a hundred. At the end of day one he was 34 not out. At the end of day two 73 not out. There was no play at all on the Saturday because of the rain, and Sunday was a rest day. On Monday he got to 97 and then got out, caught Brearley, bowled Botham, having battled through 282 balls - enough time for Buttler to score half a dozen white ball hundreds.

This infatuation was succeeded the following year by a flirtation with the whole of the Pakistan team for the 1979 World Cup, to the extent that I supported Pakistan in the game against England at Headingley. But, as always seems to be the case at Headingley, Pakistan were fairly hopeless and lost, despite only having to chase down England's lowly score of 165. Pakistan were all out for 151, with Boycott the bowler polishing off the innings and finishing with 2-14 from five overs.

A week on from the end of the Headingley test everything feels very different. The schools go back this week and it's much cooler. My son is delighted with the drop in temperature and went off for his game for the Sunday twos talking excitedly about wearing a short sleeved jumper with his long sleeved shirt, a combination, I imagine, favoured by Jos Buttler. Despite a long session yesterday afternoon with the dog thrower, he doesn't seem very confident about his chances of making any runs. 'The trouble with Sunday cricket,' he says 'is they're all grenade launchers – but accurate. Or eighty-year-olds, who used to play for Middlesex Second XI, and swing it round corners.'

He promises to text me with a rough estimate of when he'll be batting but after a couple of hours, I've heard nothing and assume his team must be fielding. To get out of any more gardening I go at what I think must be the later stages of the opposition's innings. In fact, he's batting. The opposition turned up late and he went in at number four, but he couldn't let me know because his phone had died. He's been in a while and is into the twenties. His batting partner, who I recognise as one of his friend's dads, is facing an elderly grenade launcher. After several extravagant but unsuccessful swings of his bat, he tries even harder and falls over. The next ball he hits straight up in the air and sets off for a suicidal single, and, to his obvious relief, is run out. He's replaced by the captain, who is nearly seventy, but still a prolific run scorer in Sunday cricket. He's particularly adept at stealing a single from the final ball of the over, but otherwise seems reluctant to run between the wickets. As a result, my son's innings grinds to a halt and, when he reaches 40, he's out, attempting a big swish against one of their many slow bowlers.

Monday 2 September

It's the first day of the new school year for our local schools, but only if you're a teacher. It's an Inset Day so both of my children get to stay in bed. In my son's case, I imagine his lie-in may be of some duration, given the moaning and groaning last night at bedtime, following his relatively long stay at the crease and forty overs in the field. The cricket boots, which he persuaded me at the start of the season were 'absolutely essential' and a 'perfect fit', have left their mark again and he can barely walk this morning. His task for today was supposed to be wearing in his new school shoes – if only whilst playing on the Xbox and watching multiple episodes of *Peaky Blinders* – but I can't see that happening now.

Sure enough, when I get home in the afternoon, he still hasn't got round to putting his socks on. But he has tidied up his desk and fished out his school books from beneath the piles of cricket magazines. One of these now has pride of place on the shelf above his desk – *The Cricketer* magazine's World Cup edition, the one with guess who on the cover.

Tuesday 3 September

Only the new Year 7s and Year 12s are required to attend my son's school today. Despite his sore feet he drags himself off the sofa to join some of his friends at the nets in the afternoon. School and his GCSEs will demand his attention from tomorrow but he seems determined to hang on to summer for as long as possible and gives me a full cricketing round-up in the car on the way home, apparently oblivious to the dramatic events unfolding at Westminster, which I had been trying to follow on the radio. Jofra (with whom he's also now on first name terms) has been bowling left arm spin to Jos in the nets at Old Trafford, who has also been batting left-handed. His own batting allegedly included almost taking his friend's head off with a Buttler-style flat straight six, and he tells me he also played a number of scoops. And it is forecast to rain on Thursday (day two), he adds with some satisfaction. I am not working on Thursdays this year and had been looking forward to watching the cricket – though it turns out later that this was a wind-up. And Bumble says there are quite a few heavy cracks on the pitch, which should interest the pace bowlers. Without the option of Anderson, England have selected big burly Craig Overton instead of Chris Woakes. My son is happy as this brings the total of Somerset players in the team to three. Buttler is technically a Lancashire player and, despite my son confidently predicting he will re-join 'Leachy' and Somerset next year, has just been awarded a new contract, although for what is not clear. Because of the World Cup he's not played a single game for them this year and probably won't play for them at all, unless Lancashire make it to finals day for the 20/20 Blast.

Fourth Test: Old Trafford

4-8 September

Wednesday 4 September

After Headingley, the Old Trafford test gets off to a terrible start. There is play in the morning, but after two quick wickets, England hit the combined brick wall of Steve Smith and his apprentice, Australia's new number three Marnus Labuschagne. Despite this having been my son's first day back at school, he seems very well-informed about the morning session, the result he says of watching it on his phone during break and at lunchtime. He assures me that he wasn't watching it during his lessons. It wasn't a session worth risking getting caught watching on your phone.

There is a long break for rain in the afternoon session but by the time we get home from school the covers have been taken off and play resumes at four o'clock. It's very windy and looks freezing. Jofra Archer, who starts after the break, looks extremely reluctant to peel off his two jumpers and when he does finally bowl, his first delivery is a harmless loosener, clocked at only 77mph.

To the question, 'Can he recall seeing a crowd look colder at a test match', my son offers the Headingley test against New Zealand at the end of May 2015, in which, he adds, Buttler scored a battling seventy on the last day in a lost cause. Today the TV cameras show him employing hand warmers between deliveries.

On the plus side, my son enjoys the spectacle of the players wearing their long-sleeved jumpers. At one point the wind is so strong that the umpires give up on the bails and play without them. A beach ball flying across the playing area is the highlight of a short session. After a few overs they go off again for rain but are back out almost immediately when it stops and the sun comes out, briefly. But at tea it tips down and play is abandoned for the day.

Thursday 5 September

There is a brief and rather desperate attempt by my son this morning to pull a sickie. When I take him up a piece of toast, he claims to have hit his head in the night. This is a variation on earache, his tried and tested method, and reflects that he knows nothing will work so early in the school year.

In the penultimate week of the summer term I had colluded in his absence from school / watching films so that he could watch the World Cup semi-final against Australia. On that occasion he had been sufficiently nervous not to blame England's top order for knocking off the runs and had been happy for events to depart from his usual game plan, which involves them getting out and making way for Buttler to bat. For once he had concentrated on the big picture and celebrated the team's thumping eight wicket win and a place in the final on Sunday. Happily, his own team made a mess of their run-chase, in the match which would have sent them to the under-fourteen county finals on the same Sunday, and we were able to bear witness to the drama from Lords, together in front of the TV.

The final week of the school year and the start of the summer holiday were then the perfect opportunity to replay and reflect on what had happened. Inevitably his analysis offered a different narrative to the one in the newspapers and on TV. Buttler, in this revisionist account, was at least equal in heroism to Stokes, and had arguably sacrificed his wicket in the face of scoreboard pressure, partly created by Stokes' inability to rotate the strike. Only Buttler, in the match, had managed to score at a run a ball on a horrible pudding of a pitch. Without the outrageous good fortune England enjoyed in the 50th over, New Zealand would have won, the man of the match award might well have gone to the slow-medium pacer, Colin de Grandhomme, for achieving the miserly figures of 10-2-25-1, and the new groundsman might well have got the sack for preparing such a duff surface.

An old work colleague, who has celebrated his escape from teaching by becoming a steward at Lords, told me that the atmosphere in the ground changed as soon as Buttler came out to bat. When Morgan was out, it was Buttler who got England going again, through a combination of wristy quick singles and powerful drives through the off side. His innings also included the two shots of the day – the ramp shot which went for four down to the members pavilion and the ramp shot which became a delicate sweep for two when Lockie Ferguson anticipated his intentions and bowled a fast, straight Yorker. But when Buttler was out, my friend said, the utter deflation my son and I experienced in front of the TV at home, had been shared in the Grandstand, where he was stationed.

Later in the day, as the ground emptied, he spotted David Cameron coming down from the safety of one of the private boxes. Even in the warm afterglow of World Cup victory, Brexit hadn't been forgotten and he watched as one man advanced, offered his hand to the former Prime Minister, and then called him a 'bloody pillock'.

As it had been for England's players, the World Cup had been an exhausting few weeks for the President of the Jos Buttler Appreciation Society. School continually got in the way of the cricket and there had also been his own form and trigger movements to worry about. Apparently, the addition of a new pair of cricket boots, from a firm called Payntr, would provide greater stability and balance at the crease. I suspect this may have been a cunning attempt at reverse psychology: I would be grateful he wasn't asking for the more expensive New Ballance spikes worn by Buttler and most of the other big names, and would, therefore, submit more readily to the cheaper option he was offering. The new boots didn't, however, stop him running himself out in his first appearance of the season for the men's Saturday fourth XI. Somehow, he had failed to spot that his batting partner was a fifty something accountant, not a spry under-fourteen; having called for an impossible second run, he was sent back in no uncertain terms, slipped, and was run out by miles.

The other equipment issue, I'd been avoiding all of last year, was a new bag. His old one couldn't be worn like an enormous rucksack on your back, as favoured by international players as they head off to the nets, and so was deemed a write-off. But its replacement – a suspiciously cheap one from Grey-and-Nicolls – wasn't quite what he'd had in mind either. Forty pounds was a bargain, but it also only bought him a very small bag to put on his back. There wasn't room in it, for example, for his new boots, which led a charmed life at the start of May, being left behind in various cricket pavilions around Hertfordshire.

There were no such problems for England at the start of their World Cup campaign, which started with a convincing win against South Africa at the Oval. There was then a malfunction in the script for the next match against Pakistan, which England lost despite hundreds from Root and Buttler (103 from 76 balls), but it was assumed this wouldn't stop them progressing to the semi-finals. They beat Bangladesh comfortably in the next match at Cardiff with Roy and Bairstow leading the charge, but that was overshadowed in our house by the more serious matter of Buttler's hip – which he appeared to injure hitting a ball into the River Taff.

Fortunately, he had nearly a week to recover for the next match against the West Indies, another comfortable win. A bit too comfortable for my son's liking, because it meant Buttler didn't bat. And the same happened against Afghanistan, so that when he came out against Sri Lanka, with England making a mess of chasing a modest target, it felt like Buttler was suddenly a bit out of rhythm and form.

My son was also finding himself short of time in the middle, although for different reasons. He, and a couple of other under-fourteens playing for the Saturday fourth XI, weren't just used to make up the numbers and run around in the outfield. To his credit, the captain gave them all plenty of chance to bat or bowl, but it was a steep learning curve. In the second match of the season my son batted at four and texted, 'Got 1. LBW. Horrible quick off spinner. Plumb but a good ball. So annoying. I batted ok for 12 balls but got dragged across the stumps and he fired one in at my pads.' Then, with a hint of schadenfreude aimed at his school mate, added, 'James then got a golden.'

Without the benefit of any media training, he also isn't above making excuses when dismissed cheaply, as happened again in the next match: 'Out for 5. Bowled. Hit a 4 first ball then took a single. Then tried to pull one that died.' Press reports suggested that there had been a more honest self-assessment / clear the air team meeting after England's back-to-back losses against Sri Lanka and Australia, and it clearly did the trick. England had to beat India and New Zealand in their next two games and did exactly that.

Day two of the Old Trafford test, however, turns out to be a good day's cricket to miss. Jonathan Agnew described it as a 'chastening' day for England and by the close of play they are already batting for a draw to keep the ashes alive. The two heroes of Headingley both have days to forget. Stokes goes for more than six runs an over and breaks down in his eleventh over with a suspected shoulder injury. But Leach has an even worse day. Having had Smith caught at slip from a good ball that spun and took the outside edge, the TV ruined the celebrations by showing Leach overstepping the crease and bowling a no ball, despite him being a slow left arm spinner, who bowls off about four paces. Boycott on TMS called him a 'muppet' and had a point. Smith was only on 118 when this happened but went on to make 211.

When he got home from school my son informed me that of the 15,508 deliveries Leach has bowled in first class cricket, only two had been no balls, prior to this one. This is later contradicted on the radio by Agnew who puts Leach's career no ball count at eight.

After tea I made the mistake of suggesting that Leach looked fairly innocuous, whereupon he spun the next ball sharply and had Cummins taken by Stokes at slip. My son responded by hitting me over the head with a cushion, and repeating, 'Leave Leachy alone!' And when Smith is finally out, it's a good moment for a renewal of his vows: 'I would never switch Jos for Smith, no matter how many runs he scores.' But the day ends with England trailing by 474 and the prospect of

Buttler batting at number eight because Craig Overton was used as night watchman, following the fall of Denly.

Saturday 7 September

I was back at work / school yesterday, so I hardly saw any of the third day. The school day began with another assembly from the Head Teacher about 'resilience', during which I found my mind drifting away from the importance of homework and solving problems in class, to England's batting.

My son was delighted to find that we'd booked him a dentist appointment for two o'clock and convinced his mother that there was no point in returning to school for the last period. Because of the long rain delay in the morning, he ended up watching nearly the whole of the day's play. It finished rather nervously for him with Buttler next man in. The new ball is only six overs away and he's already worrying about his man coming in against the new conker or brand-new cherry, as Shane Warne likes to say on commentary.

It is slightly mortifying to reflect that, at the age of 52, the success or otherwise of the weekend rests on Buttler making some runs today and my son doing the same for the Sunday twos tomorrow. He could also have played today for the fourth XI. Somebody dropped out this morning and the captain rang to see if he could play, which was the cue for frantic hand signals from the sofa to indicate I should make his excuses. Rather than explain that with Buttler due in next he wasn't prepared to leave the living room, I made up something about him meeting his friends.

When Bairstow is bowled playing an airy drive to a Mitchell Starc in-swinger, Buttler comes out to join Stokes. To avoid the anxiety in the living room I re-locate to the kitchen and busy myself preparing lunch – potato and leek soup – with the cricket on the radio. Normally I find something very reassuring about making potato and leek soup, but nerves get the better of me this morning and I drop the olive oil and mixed herbs in quick succession. My wife has sensed the tense hush in the house and keeps asking if Buttler's still in. Stokes doesn't last long, and when Archer is caught behind there's a disgruntled shout of, 'This is why Buttler shouldn't be batting at seven!'

Inspired by the superstitious antics of the England players in the dressing room in the closing stages at Headingley, I keep to the kitchen and TMS whilst Buttler is on strike, and then shoot to the living room for the deliveries to Stuart Broad or replays of boundaries. The radio commentary is about five seconds ahead of what he is watching. A very tight Buttler leave, which induces panic in the TMS commentary box, is spun from the sofa as, 'Heck of a leave that.'

Buttler is still there at lunch on 26 not out, and, for my son, there is the tantalising prospect of Somerset chums Buttler and Leach batting together after the break. At 1.56 Broad is cleaned-up by Starc and there is a whoop of joy from the living room. 'Leachy and Jos!' Leach is given a huge ovation and the TV cameras pick out a group of Leaches in the crowd – sporting thick-rimmed glasses, Spec-saver T-shirts, and wearing what appear to be enormous condoms stretched over their heads to simulate Leach's bald head.

When Leach plays a couple of solid defensive shots my son starts to get greedy and dream of a Buttler hundred, whereupon he's bowled for 41, attempting to hit Cummins back over his head.

Sunday 8 September

My son greets me at breakfast with the news that it is forecast to rain for three of the next four day in Manchester, only not today. It was so cold last night that I had to put the heating on for a bit, and parts of the UK have apparently woken up this morning to a touch of frost, but, perversely, the sun is shining in Manchester. It's also Buttler's birthday today, he informs me.

England have got to bat for something like 98 overs if they are to escape with a draw. Burns and Root went to successive deliveries from Cummins last night, so Roy and Denly are the unlikely first pairing who will be trying to bat time.

By the time Buttler's in, soon after lunch, I have the living room and the sofa to myself. My son is playing for the Sunday men's team. He texts to tell me they're batting and he's at six and will text when they are two down to give me time to get to the club to watch him bat. Meanwhile Bairstow and Buttler are batting well. Just before the mid-session drinks interval Australia bring on part-time spinners from both ends. This opens up the awful prospect of Buttler getting out to Marnus Labuschagne, who looks more like a Springbok scrum half than an Australian cricketer. There's something particularly unpleasant about the aggressive way he spins the ball to himself before each delivery. They make it to drinks but Bairstow is then out immediately after, LBW to Starc.

There's a rather more relaxed atmosphere up at my son's cricket club. His team are 223-3 when I arrive and, when he goes in next, I am able to watch him and Buttler simultaneously –

him through the window and Buttler on the big screen in the clubhouse. My son looks to have been stumped when he's on 2, but the square leg umpire is one of his school friends and annoys the opposition by giving him not out. He then survives a confident LBW appeal to the same umpire, by which time I decide I need a drink. A change of ball in Manchester suddenly produces conventional swing and has Buttler groping for the ball during a Cummins over in which he hardly lays bat on ball. This happened at Edgbaston in the first test and then it also coincided with Buttler's short innings.

Having hit a four to leg, my son attempts to touch gloves with his batting partner – a grey haired man well into his fifties. He ignores my son's outstretched hand and pats him on the back instead. At 267-4 he runs past a slow dobber and is stumped for 10, at which point I decide to return to my vigil on the sofa. Buttler has survived a sharp in-ducker from Cummins, which hit his pads, and is still there at tea.

At 4.44 pm my son rings to tell me he's done his groin in, going down to make a long barrier, and can I come and pick him up because he's no longer able to field. My first thought is that he might be faking the injury to get out of fielding in order to watch Buttler bat, but this becomes irrelevant three minutes later when Buttler shoulders arms and is bowled by an in-swinger from Hazelwood.

There is still the unlikely prospect of a Somerset rear guard from Overton and Leach, who has been promoted to number ten. As soon as we get home my son puts his lucky cap on and starts crossing off the balls that still have to be faced on a piece of paper. They survive for over an hour, but it's not to be. Leach falls to Labuschagne and Hazelwood traps Overton LBW to retain the Ashes.

Monday 9 September

My son has been picking over the bones of yesterday's defeat. His usual post-match ritual involves listening to various podcasts for their analysis of Buttler's performance and his chances of being picked for the next match. Dominic Cork, on Sky's Cricket Debate, has upset him by suggesting that Roy be retained for the final test at the Oval, at Buttler's expense – obviously an absurd suggestion, and thankfully not one that's in tune with the selectors, who name an unchanged squad for the final test. Only the *Wisden* podcast properly recognises the quality of Buttler's batting at Old Trafford and it has him purring in agreement when he plays it to me in the kitchen after school. There's also Steve Smith to feel angry with for his imitation of Leach in the post-match celebrations, which according to *The Times* consisted of wiping a pair of glasses before putting them on and shadow batting left-handed.

He's also begun campaigning to be taken to the Oval, and is targeting Thursday – my day off, but not his, I have to remind him. And the only tickets available seem to involve obscure online ticket agencies and vastly inflated prices.

A more serious obstacle to watching any cricket, let alone taking a day off school and going to the Oval, is the arrival of his grandparents / my in-laws for their annual visit. They don't exactly live around the corner, and so tend to descend for a long stretch when they come. Neither do they have any interest in cricket. There is talk of doing something at the weekend – an excursion / day out of some sort. My son has just realised the danger and is busy making plans to do his Art project at a friend's house who has Sky Sports.

By a cruel twist of fate, we were staying with them in the summer of 2018 when Buttler scored his first, and, so far, only test match hundred. It was the last day of our stay, and my son and I spent the day on their sofa watching the cricket from Trent Bridge on his phone, which they clearly regarded as bizarre behaviour.

Fortunately, Buttler raced through the nervous nineties, but overall it had been a hard-fought innings against excellent bowling, and runs had come fairly slowly by his standards. Stokes, at the other end, was considerably slower, and in very scratchy form compared to his batting this summer. When Buttler clipped a four behind square to reach his hundred, my son went down on his knees to offer thanks to the almighty. There were also words of thanks for Ed Smith, the new Chairman of Selectors, who earlier in the summer had brought Buttler back from the IPL and into the test squad for the two-match series against Pakistan.

As it turned out, James Whittaker might have done Buttler a favour by not selecting him for the winter tour. The Ashes series proved to be a good one for him to miss and there had also been the silver lining of the sandpaper down Bancroft's pants in South Africa. The defeat to Australia was quickly forgotten, and instead of Steve Smith – now banned – Buttler would be the main man for the Rajistan Royals in the IPL, equalling Virender Sehwag's record of five successive scores of fifty or more. Unlike the Bangladesh Premier League, into which Buttler had vanished from view the previous autumn, all of the IPL matches were available on Sky or ITV, and my son spent the month of May in a permanent state of nervous excitement - evident in the regular score updates he texted me every time I wasn't available to join him on the sofa in front of the TV.

Delhi Capitals v Rajistan Royals (2 May 2018)

19.01 Jos opening. 12 over game. Will text u how he does.

19.14 Wow. He's putting on a show. Just ramped Boult for 6. 25 off 9 balls.

19.16 OMG. Now on 36 off 12. 23 from last over.

19.22 Omggg. Just reverse swept a spinner for six to get his 50 off 18 balls.

19.32 Out for 68 off 26.

22.16 Jos was heroic. He should open for England.

Chennai Super Kings v Rajistan Royals (11 May 2018)

19.19 Ohhhhhhh myyy goddd!! 8 off 2 balls and Jos hit a mega six before hitting the winning runs. 97 not outtttt!! Wow

Unfortunately, Buttler's return to test cricket last year coincided with a school day, but my son still managed to keep a close eye on events at Lords, presumably by breaking the school rules about no phones in lessons.

England v Pakistan (24 May 2018)

10.54 England batting.

12.02 33-2 Root out to a terrible shot. Cook looks solid.

12.11 43-3 Milan gone

12.13 Malan even

14.29 100-4 Bairstow bowled. Poor shot.

15.24 Jos alert. Cook out to a good ball. 140-odd for 5

15.26 Oh god. Almost played on first ball. Very poor shot but got away with it.

15.30 Jos 11 off 6 balls. Two superb fours.

Then it went strangely quiet. Buttler had chased a very wide ball at the very moment my son got home from school. Caught in the slips for a breezy 14.

There was then an anxious wait for his second innings – thankfully, a responsible rear guard of 67 from 138 balls, in partnership with the young Somerset spinner Dom Bess. No matter that England went on to lose the match by nine wickets. This was a very good result for my son / team Buttler, and it suddenly became essential for us to go to the second test at Headingley. For once his online ticket shopping stumbled on an unlikely bargain – a Yorkshire CC giveaway of two adults and one child for only £60, made possible by sitting in the family enclosure and not drinking.

At Bristol, in the ODI we had travelled some distance to the previous September, my son had seen Buttler bat for four balls and score two. At Headingley on day one, Pakistan won the toss and, most unhelpfully, chose to bat, and he didn't see him bat at all. They didn't make a great job of it and were out before tea for 174, after which we got to see Keaton Jennings bat, and the £60 suddenly didn't seem such a good deal. At the close England were 106-2, and because Bess had been sent out at the end of the day as night watchman, Buttler had slipped a place in the batting order.

When he did come out to bat, on day two, we were travelling back on the train, and by the time we caught up with him on Saturday morning Buttler was batting with the tail. The sight of Broad and Anderson walking out to bat sent him into one day mode and he hit 35 from his last 11 balls, including a huge straight six into the building site of what is now the new football stand. With a hundred in sight, Anderson offered slip catching practice to Haris Sohail, and Buttler was left stranded on 80 not out – his only innings of the match. Pakistan capitulated in their second innings and England won by an innings and Buttler was named man of the series.

Test cricket was then put on hold whilst England played a rather meaningless five match ODI series against an Australian team missing most of its best players – Warner and Smith had been banned after the sandpaper scandal and Cummins, Hazelwood and Stark were all injured. The series also had to compete with the football world cup, but not in my son's case. When one of my friends hosted a day of South American food to coincide with the England v Panama game, he refused to join me because England's cricketers – already 4-0 up in the series – had yet another ODI on the same day. His loyalty was rewarded by Buttler with an innings of 110 not out, which steered England to an unlikely victory after they'd been 114-8 chasing 206.

By the time test cricket resumed with the series against India, the heat wave, which had made school so uncomfortable in June and July, was over. *Wisden* described the atmospheric conditions which replaced it as a 'clammy blanket', perfect for swing bowling. And because everything was so dry, there was also reverse swing. For the first test at Edgbaston the groundsman attempted to preserve moisture by treating the outfield with seaweed. This didn't help Buttler, or my son, who both came down to earth with a bump with scores of 0 and 1. The wobble wasn't steadied until the third test at Trent Bridge where Buttler top scored in both innings, and scored the hundred that we watched on my son's phone at his grandparents. He got runs in the fourth test at the Rose Bowl, and 89 on his birthday in the final test at the Oval. One of my friend's fiftieth birthday presents had been four tickets to the Saturday of the Oval test – for which I, but not my son, controversially, was selected. Inevitably, Buttler got runs when my son wasn't in the vicinity and ended up as England's top scorer in the series.

During the afternoon session the television cameras / big screen showed Boris Johnson fiddling with his phone, lounging back in his seat in a private box at the Pavilion End. The Oval crowd immediately started booing, at which point he looked up with a mixture of confusion and alarm, and the Sky producers cut to something else before the atmosphere turned even nastier – not unlike the moment in 1989 when the Romanian people turned on the dictator Nicolae Ceausescu as he addressed a huge rally in Bucharest, and the state TV channel panicked and went off air.

Unlike Johnson, who'd gone to ground for a bit following his resignation in July as Foreign Secretary, Buttler, to my son's delight, was everywhere – at least in the magazines and on the podcasts that mattered to him. A particular favourite was the Sky Sports feature in which Ian Ward travelled to Buttler's old school – the Kings School in Taunton. The cricket facilities Buttler had enjoyed looked very much like those at the local independent school my son's team had played earlier in the season, then as under 13s. They had also had a cricket professional and a chapel beyond the cricket field. And the sandwiches the school provided were so sophisticated that none of my son's team would touch them. Rather than risk avocado with chicken and bacon they made straight for the chocolate cake before taking the field in apologetic fashion to defend their modest score against the best under-13 batsman in the county. There was none of the inclusive nonsense his team were used to, with batsmen retiring when they reached thirty; the star player was allowed to keep going, finishing with 65 not out and hitting the runs off in nine brutal overs.

To his credit, this particular boy appeared completely unconscious of his superiority, and behaved impeccably whilst destroying the opposition. My memory of taking the senior sides to play public schools in the 1990s and early 2000s was of a rather different breed of boy than I was used to – evident in the precocious small talk of the captain as he met his opposite number or spoke to the visiting member of staff, and the tedious insouciance and sledging of the mini David Gowers in the slips. And when we travelled east from London to the Essex public schools, there were the old Essex county pros lying in wait – the unsmiling Scot, Brian Hardie, at Brentwood, and the ultra-competitive Stuart Turner at Forest School, Nasser Hussain's old school.

Conscious as we were of the rather inferior environment, we (a boys' comprehensive school) could offer as the home-team, it didn't help when a gaggle of geese set up camp on the first XI cricket square. Before every home fixture it was necessary to allow time for clearing up goose shit before the opposition arrived. The only receptacle I could find for this in the old score hut was a silver platter, and on one occasion the introductions were made with the visiting school whilst I was still holding it, piled high with goose droppings.

Tuesday 10 September

When I went into my son's room this morning, he appeared to be fast asleep, and his phone was emitting soothing water noises – presumably the same sleep-inducing App he had heard Steve Smith mention in his post-match interviews at Manchester. It's a welcome change from the Flintoff and Robbie Savage podcast, but also quite unnecessary. Unlike Steve Smith he doesn't have to worry about the pressure of test match cricket and sleeps perfectly well. Obviously, he's been prepared to overlook the matter of Smith's meanness to Jack Leach, in favour of a good night's sleep.

Even in his comatose state, he's still first to today's big cricketing story and greets me with, 'You know Boycott's been given a knighthood.'

Later in the day the Australian coach, Justin Langer, clears up the glasses story. Smith was actually giving a heads up to the former Australian opener Chris Rogers, 'a good mate of the squad'. As if.

Wednesday 11 September

On several occasions over the past few days I have been approached by my son holding the Xbox controls, as if it were a cricket bat, and asked to adjudicate on two different versions of his batting stance, or 'set-up' as he likes to call it. I probably haven't paid very much attention, and have struggled to see any difference between them.

He repeated the question this evening when I was giving him some throw-downs on the patio in the back garden. (There is, currently, a patio cricket ban in place following damage to an outside light and numerous plants and flowers, but I decided it was a sacrifice worth making to get him away from the Xbox and *Red Dead Redemption 2*). This time, one version was clearly an imitation of Steve Smith, which I pointed out bordered on unpatriotic, and rather like jumping ship now that the Ashes were gone, and urged him to stick with the second option, modelled on the young Somerset batsman Tom Banton. Alternatively, I could have reminded him of one of the key messages from interviews with his hero – the importance of being 'the best version of yourself' – but I decided to leave that for another day. We managed to get through the session on the patio without any breakages and without arguing. I was throwing the tennis ball from only about twelve yards away, so it was important, he told me, not to rush him – 'Give me time to get my trigger in.'

Fifth Test: Oval

12-16 September

Thursday 12 September

Very decently my wife took her parents out on a long walk this morning, and I had the house and the TV to myself. It's a gorgeous day at the Oval, and when Tim Paine chose to bowl first on a seemingly flat pitch, my mind cast back to 1985, when Gooch and Gower batted all day and put England into an unassailable position. Expectations are a bit lower today. When the score reaches 11 for no wicket, thanks to a streaky boundary from Denly – from a delivery he was actually attempting to leave – David Lloyd cheerily informs viewers that England have exceeded the average opening stand in this series.

Denly's is the only wicket to fall in a very quiet morning session. So quiet that I fall asleep, briefly, and miss Root being dropped at square leg by Peter Siddle, which feels like a window into a possible life after school teaching / in retirement. There is no need to worry – Root is dropped twice more, either side of lunch.

My son had gone off to school this morning without whinging too much, or any last-minute talk of feeling unwell, and his stoicism is rewarded with an evening session to savour. Root falls to Cummins, just as he is settling himself on the sofa after school, and just as the ball starts to swing and, as a result, the start of Buttler's innings is not without some scary moments. When he's on one, Boycott gives him out on the radio following a confident shout for a catch to the wicket keeper down the leg side, but this is overruled by my son in the living room, who has unshakeable faith and the benefit of the TV replays. Buttler is then struck a painful blow – a short ball from Hazelwood which cannons off his chest up into his face. It's fair to say the bowler appears rather less concerned about this than my son, although it's hard to know / lip read with Hazelwood, who has a very small mouth, not unlike a ventriloquist's dummy. This seems to sting Buttler into action, or it could simply be that he's been joined by Jack Leach again, who has a first-class average of 11. Hazelwood is hit for successive straight sixes and then he attempts a ramp shot which doesn't come off. My son pleads with him to bat more sensibly but Buttler continues in one day mode until the new ball is taken for the last two overs of the day. At the close he is 64 not out and Leach is also still there, and all is right with the world.

Friday 13 September

A line from a Larkin poem – one about the 'certainty of time laid up in store' – springs to mind ahead of the morning session. I have already taught a double lesson by the time Buttler and Leach go out to bat, and what would otherwise have been a dull morning feels lifted by the hope of their partnership continuing. To keep this hope alive, I make no attempt to check the score in the two periods after morning break, and only check BBC Sport at the start of the lunch break at 12.45, only to find that Australia are batting and Smith and Labuschagne are the not out batsmen. Buttler only added six runs to his overnight score and was out attempting a rash shot to a straight ball from the remorseless Cummins.

Smith is still there at half past three when I put the car radio on at the end of the school day, but Australia have lost another couple of wickets and there is hope we might be able to bowl everyone else out and have a decent first innings lead. He's not been at his best according to TMS, and has looked 'human' Michael Vaughan says, which is slightly contradicted, later on, by reports that he's got flu but is still comfortably Australia's top scorer. Mercifully he misses the first ball of Woakes' spell after tea – a slow-ish, straight loosener – and is out LBW for 80. At the close, England have a lead of 78, and survive a couple of hostile overs from Cummins and Hazelwood without losing a wicket.

Saturday 14 September

Somehow, I've ended up doing the netball run for my daughter and her friend. It's an eleven o'clock meet for an eleven thirty start, so instead of doing the shopping first thing and then rewarding myself with the morning session, I am sat in Wormley watching netball. But having used my children's various commitments to ward off the threat of a whole day outing with my in-laws, I can't really complain. Unfortunately, my daughter's position is Goalkeeper, which seems to consist of static and ultimately doomed attempts to put off the opposition Goal Shooter, and then making conversation with them when the play is up the other end.

An alternative course of action would have been to disregard any thoughts of domestic harmony and accept the offer, made late last night from an old colleague, of a free ticket for today at the Oval. But with the in-laws here, and my son still smarting from his miserable day at Lords, that was never really an option.

My son is also missing at least the first hour of play, having very reluctantly allowed himself to be prised from the sofa so he can see a physiotherapist about his stiff groin.

England's plan for the day, by general consent, is just to bat all day. If they're still batting at the close, they'll win, according to Alec Stewart on TMS. Encouragingly, he gives Australia a one percent chance of chasing down a score in excess of 350. Meanwhile, my cunning plan involves taking my in-laws to a local farm-turned-restaurant for a cream tea in the afternoon. This will have the appearance of an outing but should only take about an hour out of the day's play. And by leaving as the players come off for tea, I end up missing a bit less than an hour.

Before tea / cream tea, England were advancing without alarm, with both Denly and Stokes well set. By the time we get home they and Bairstow are out and Buttler is batting with Sam Curran. My son is nervously shadow batting with the Xbox controls in the living room, unable to sit down. He tells me he's been chewing the same bit of now tasteless chewing gum since Buttler came to the crease and is sticking with it whilst he remains. Buttler is on 23.

Instead of doing the Art homework he's been set, a new World Cup-themed collage / homage is taking shape in my son's sketchbook, which is open on the coffee table. Of the four completed pieces of work he's managed since the start of last year, three have featured Jos Buttler and one was an outline of Viv Richards.

Just when it seemed he'd have the luxury of Buttler not out overnight for the second time in the match, Buttler is caught by the pesky Labuschagne, running forward at deep square leg to take a brilliant catch. Disappointing, but with scores of 70 and now 47, my son can afford to be philosophical – 'At least he's now averaging more than Bairstow for the series.'

Sunday 15 September

The one benefit of Buttler getting out last night is that my son is happy to go to his guitar lesson at ten o'clock. It would have been nice for him to bat on this morning, but hopefully England have a big enough lead. More pertinently from my son's point of view, Buttler has finished the series strongly, arrested the decline in his batting average, and booked his place in the team for the tours to New Zealand and South Africa.

Our conversation in the car on the way to his lesson is an earnest discussion of The Hundred – the new limited over competition being introduced next year. He is torn between wanting Buttler to be a leading figure in the new tournament, and worrying about his hectic schedule, and reads me the England fixtures for next summer from his phone. For some reason this involves another visit from Australia to play more One Day Internationals. Their appearance last summer (2018) for five ODIs was unwarranted, although at least it could be argued that it was part of England's preparation for the World Cup. But coming again next year, and so soon after the World Cup and the Ashes is, we both agree, completely barmy.

Almost as soon as we set off for home after his lesson, Archer is caught down the leg side. Broad hits a couple of sixes – attacking Cummins' short balls, Agnew says, like a man hacking down a tree – but then Leach is caught as soon as he attempts an aggressive shot. Australia need 400, exactly, to win.

During the changeover my passenger reflects complacently on what, for him, has 'been a pleasing test match…Bairstow failed, Buttler scored runs. Just need Leach to get a six for.'

In this relaxed mood he's happy to cast his eye over other contenders for the winter tours and starts quoting Sam North-East's statistics in the county championship.

We are home in time to see Broad's first over to Warner. The assumption is that Warner will fall cheaply again, but there's the horrible thought – encouraged by some of the Australian ex-players / commentators – that it might be his day. When Broad has him caught in the slips for 11, it sounds as if Shane Warne has been rehearsing his own cheesy send-off: 'Broad's been all over Warner like a cheap suit!' Labuschagne also goes cheaply for once, stumped off Leach and stomps off towards the pavilion arguing with himself, as seems to be his way.

And then at 85-4, in the twenty seventh over, Smith is out for a mere 23, caught appropriately in a bodyline-style leg trap from the bowling of a Nottinghamshire pace bowler, Stuart Broad. Which just leaves Matthew Wade as the last of the specialist batsmen / unpleasant combative Aussies. He's been particularly punchy under the helmet at short leg all through the series and is clearly not very popular with the England players. At tea he walks off exchanging insults with Ben Stokes but is still there and scoring quickly. The thought of Wade doing a Stokes is horrible and drives me out of the living room after tea. Perhaps if I go and do something else entirely, everything will slot into place.

In 2009 at the Oval there had been the more realistic prospect of Ricky Ponting and Michael Hussey doing something special, and batting Australia to an improbable victory. That had been a similarly hot day and dry pitch, and my coping strategy had involved ignoring the cricket for stretches of twenty minutes, or longer if I could hold out, and then turning the car radio on hoping for a wicket. The passenger, on that occasion, had been my grandmother, who I had gone to collect from her home in Bromley. Like the friend, in whose garden I seek refuge today after tea, my grandmother had no interest in cricket, but had managed to be politely enthusiastic when I turned on TMS just as Flintoff ran out Ponting, and immediately after Strauss did the same to Michael Clarke.

My son rings to tell me that Archer is bowling really fast to Wade, but that's not really what I want to hear. Wade has got his hundred by the time I get home, and I am conscious of being slightly tetchy on the phone when an old friend rings at about the time that runs needed are down to about 150. He tells me not to be absurd, that England will win easily. Almost immediately after, Cummins edges a ball from Broad and is caught behind. England don't have to dismiss the obdurate Siddle because Wade runs past a spinning ball from Root and is stumped. Lyon and Hazelwood are out to successive deliveries in Leach's next over and England have won. Leach only has a 4 for, but Buttler has taken a sharp catch and my son has every reason to be satisfied. My friend rang at the fall of Hazelwood's wicket to say, 'I told you so.'

Ten minutes after the end of the match, I returned to the living room to find my son playing on the Xbox. I assumed he'd still be watching the cricket for the interviews and analysis. 'I would,' he says, 'but I don't want to watch them (Australia) lifting the Ashes.'

In the evening my wife rather pointedly reclaims the living room and the TV and announces that she's watching what she wants for once. Now that the result isn't in doubt, I would like to watch the highlights of the bits of the day I missed or avoided, but that will have to wait until tomorrow. It's a relief that the match isn't going into another day and there is a strong end of term feeling about the closing reports after the match. At midnight on Radio 4, England's win comes after Brexit, the drone strikes on Saudi Arabia's oil plants, the Lib Dem conference and another day of violent clashes in Hong Kong, but is clearly the one story the newsreader enjoys reading. There is also an end of term report on the England team's performance from the BBC's Sports Editor – for which he awards the team something like an A- / B+ for winning the World Cup and levelling the series with Australia.

The End of Summer

Wednesday 18 September

Today, after school, just as we were sitting down to a bowl of his grandmother's mushroom soup (she's still here), my son said, 'Can we talk about cricket?' as if the subject had never come up between us before. The test series might be over and the big names finally getting a break, but there are still important matters to be decided, and discussed. Tom Banton, the young Somerset batsman, and one of Buttler's understudies in his affections, failed for the second time in the match as Somerset slipped up against Hampshire. They are still in the hunt for their first ever county championship and will now have a nervy showdown against Essex their closest rivals, which he thinks will be on Sky. The much less attractive Warwickshire batsman Dominic Sibley has just scored a double century and is one of the batsmen being talked about as an alternative to England's current top six, and therefore a potential threat to Buttler's place in the team. Various commentators have repeated the line that he scores hundreds, as if there hasn't been a long line of players who have scored heavily in county cricket and then failed to do it in test cricket.

Saturday 21 September

The Sunday twos are still rolling on and my son is playing tomorrow. He requests a confidence boosting net session this morning, but it doesn't really go to plan. He hasn't played for two weeks and is as rusty as the colour of the outfield, which is now much browner and drier than it was at any point during July and August. Confusingly the oak tree next to the nets has shed its acorns. If memory serves me correctly, the Ladybird book *What to look for in Autumn* featured on its cover a squirrel foraging in dank woodland amongst brown leaves and acorns. And there were toadstools. Today the approach to the wicket is over a crunchy carpet of acorn shells in blazing sunshine. The more serious Saturday League teams have finished for the season and the only other sign of sporting life is a hockey team that is using the clubhouse as their changing room.

Perhaps all of this combines to confuse my son, who, by his own admission, appears to have forgotten how to bat. The vexed question of his head position comes up again, and his trigger movements also seem to be malfunctioning. The effect of following the Ashes so closely seems to be that he too is now getting himself trapped on the crease, Joe Root-style, except that he's only facing me with the dog thrower, not Pat Cummins. Things are so bad by the end that the best advice for tomorrow is to just forget the net session ever happened and go into bat with the expletive on Buttler's bat handle as his mantra.

The day after the world-wide climate change protests, the 20/20 finals day at Edgbaston is being played on a wicket that looks as if it belongs in Karachi or Lahore. Pace off the ball and bowling into the dusty surface will be the order of the day. In the first semi-final, the Nottingham Outlaws somehow fail to score the seven runs they require from the final over. In a replay of the super over in the World Cup Final, it comes down to three needed from two deliveries, and one side only needing a tie. Duckett only needs a single from the final ball but fails to make contact and Worcestershire go through to the final.

Their captain Moeen Ali has just announced that he's taking a break from red ball cricket, having lost his place in the test team and, it was revealed this week, also his central contract. But today he looks back to his best with bat and ball, although it helps that no one is bowling anywhere near 90mph, and the pitch is also very spin friendly. My son is supporting Worcester in the final against Essex because Moeen is Buttler's chess partner when they are on international duty, and also because Buttler's dad is from Worcestershire, he thinks. It goes down to the final ball but Essex win.

This just leaves the conclusion of the county championship next week. According to my son's weather app there's supposed to be a tropical rainstorm, by the name of Humberto, hitting Taunton on Monday and Tuesday, and then light rain on Wednesday. This isn't going to help Somerset, who need to beat Essex if they are to win their first title. Essex have a twelve-point lead going into the final game and will be quite happy if it rains for three days.

Sunday 22 September

My son greets me this morning with details from the dream he had last night – a bad dream in which his younger sister and I were at the first test of an Ashes series, in Brisbane, when Buttler made a double hundred, but for which he'd been left behind in England for poor behaviour.

When I drop him off for his match this afternoon, it looks as if storm Humberto has arrived ahead of schedule. The sky has darkened, and the atmosphere recalls the 'clammy cement' of last August. He texts me to tell me his side are batting first. He's batting at five and will text me when a couple of wickets have fallen. Shortly after they are due to start it starts raining heavily – heavily enough, I assume, for them to call it off, and so I get back in the car and drive back to the club.

By the time I get there, the rain has slowed to a steady drizzle, and they are removing the covers. A member of the home team is dragging a wheelie bin out to the middle, from which he empties a large pile of sawdust. And play resumes.

The seventy-year old run-machine notches up yet another half-century, despite the fielding side's rather desperate attempt to play mind games with him when he's on 49. The field comes in close to stop the single, but he knocks it to a fielder nearly as old as himself and makes it safely to the other end – and keeps the strike. But in the next over, when his partner dabs the ball behind point into the outfield, there's a shout of, 'Two Dave. Just two – that's all I'm running!'

The only wicket to fall is a sneaky stumping / run-out by the wicket keeper, who is standing back to the various slow bowlers, but lobs the ball at the stumps when he sees the batsman stray out of his crease. This brings out the slow scoring accountant, who always seems to be batting when I am hoping to watch my son bat. But neither he nor the elderly captain are going anywhere. Even when he's given out by his teammate, who is umpiring - presumably a thin edge to the wicket keeper – the accountant refuses to budge, and the opposition diplomatically withdraw their appeal. And then on 164-1, a young leg spinner, who's just come on to bowl, attempts to Mankad him, to the embarrassment of all concerned. His appeal isn't so much withdrawn as ignored.

I am sitting under a tree, as far from the clubhouse as I can get – encouraged by my son's unenthusiastic response to my arrival: 'You might as well go back. I won't be in for ages.' I imagine he'll be telling his fellow under-fourteen player about Ravi Ashwin's infamous Mankading of Buttler in the match between Kings XI and Rajasthan in this year's IPL. Even though it looked as if Ashwin had deliberately lured him out of his crease, pretending to go into his action but then stopping to break the wickets, Buttler didn't have the option, as happened today, of laughing it off with a 'Behave, will you' and getting on with the game.

The visiting team never do dismiss the slow scoring accountant. The elderly captain is eventually run out trying to steal a single from the last ball of an over, but no more wickets fall until a mix-up and run out on the last ball of the innings. My son – the next man in - has had his pads on for the last hour and a half but won't get to find out if yesterday's net session was an aberration, or a more serious loss of form.

* * *

I return for what I think must be the final stages and with the visitors on 156-5 chasing 218. It is nearly dark which must contribute to the home team's off spinner taking a hat-trick almost as soon as I arrive – 156-8. The next man in has to be hurriedly helped on with his pads by one of his teammates, all of which takes valuable time and means it's even darker by the time he gets out to the middle. He joins, what appears in the gloom, to be the archetypal batting blacksmith, who is 41 not out and somehow seeing the ball like a football. He proceeds to hit the ball to all parts and take his team home to an unlikely victory.

Monday 23 September

In the car on the way home from school, my son confesses to having snuck out of double English this afternoon, in order to check the England squads for New Zealand in the peace and quiet of the boys' toilets. His sister feigned disgust but can't really have been surprised given how long he spends in residence in the bathroom whilst checking his phone.

His big news is that the Buttler / Bairstow (and sometimes Foakes) conundrum has been solved in favour of Buttler. Bairstow has been left out of the test squad altogether, and from ending the series in Sri Lanka in the winter with three specialist wicket keepers in the team, the selectors have lurched the other way – there's only going to be Buttler, with Ollie Pope as cover. There is also the extra bonus of baby Buttler – the young Somerset batsman Tom Banton – being included in the 20/20 squad.

At Taunton, it has rained for much of the day, although there was still time, unfortunately, for Banton to get out for 0. Somewhat unrealistically, my son asks if I 'fancy going (to Taunton) on Wednesday'.

Tuesday 24 September

A day of torrential rain and the Supreme Court's ruling that the prorogation of Parliament was unlawful. Nevertheless, when I pick my son up after school, he still manages to immediately turn the conversation to cricket. Apparently, the weather isn't so bad in Taunton, and he's looking forward to watching Jack Leach 'turning it square'. But by the time we get home it has started raining again in Somerset, and that will be it for the day.

But on his phone, cricket is getting involved with the day's big story. Lady Hale, who read out the Supreme Court's judgement, is being portrayed on social media as Stuart Broad to Boris Johnson's David Warner. Another picture shows Lady Hale as Ben Stokes in the World Cup Final, sticking out his / her bat to inadvertently propel the fielder's return to the third man boundary, watched by a despairing Boris Johnson / New Zealand wicket keeper. Lady Hale's words have also been spliced with the voice of an irate West Indian commentator asking, 'Why did he do that? Unbelievable!' – words which were originally aimed at Shannon Gabriel, the big fast bowler, after he attempted a huge slog and was bowled from the last ball of a test match the West Indies had been battling hard to save.

Wednesday 25 September

Before he went to sleep last night, my son asked me which one of about thirty pictures of Buttler he should use as the subject for his next GCSE Art assignment, and his first time using acrylic paints. Most of them are fairly similar and show Buttler playing various attacking shots. The only other pictures in his gallery are one of Kevin Pietersen, raising his bat having got to fifty or a hundred, and one of Tom Banton. The Pietersen one might be a good choice, I suggest, because it has Mitchell Johnson with his droopy moustache glaring at him in the background, but I sense this isn't the direction he wants to go in. Clearly the choice is between Buttler or Banton, which is interesting, and it occurs to me I might be witnessing a gradual changing of the guard. Could Tom Banton soon be the new man in our lives?

I had assumed Buttler would be the Catherine Parr figure – the one he would stick with up to maturity. So far, I would say that he's been moderately promiscuous in terms of hero worship, with five, and now possibly six over-achievers on his personal podium: the footballer Philippe Coutinho, James Anderson, James Holland (writer, historian and cricket enthusiast), Ben Howard (musician), Jos Buttler, and now, possibly, Tom Banton. This would place Buttler in the Catherine Howard not Catherine Parr position, which seems all wrong after the couple of seasons he's had. (Catherine Howard was beheaded after just a year as Henry VIII's fifth wife, when he suspected her of having committed adultery with her cousin.) Perhaps that's why I suggest he ignores Banton and narrows his choice down to two of the photographs of Buttler.

* * *

Even though there's been no play at all in Taunton in the championship decider, my son hasn't given up hope of Leach spinning Somerset to the win they need. There will be a pitch inspection at 4.30, he informs me when I pick him up after school, and there's still time, he assures me, for there to be a result. That looks even more unlikely when play is abandoned for the day. There's now just one day left, assuming it stays dry, for Somerset to take twenty wickets, which may be beyond even Jack Leach.

Thursday 26 September

It's the final day of the county championship. By the time play starts in Taunton it's midday, and the floodlights are already on. Leach has a very good shout for LBW in his first over, but Sir Alistair Cook is given not out, and there are no DRS reviews. At 12.05 it starts raining again and the players go off but are back on again after ten minutes.

It's a slightly confusing scene: the wicket has the dusty, dry appearance of a sub-continent surface – a raging Bunsen in cricketing parlance – but the outfield is damp and lush after several days of heavy rain. It isn't long before the Quantock Hills in the distance start to disappear behind misty low cloud and, just after 12.30, rain stops play again and the players take an early lunch.

Sky devote the lunch break to Marcus Trescothick. This is his last day of first-class cricket after a career lasting 27 years. His original county cap, which began life a dark shade of maroon, has now faded to a russet brown.

Once Cook is dismissed after lunch for 53, wickets start to fall, and there is a faint hope that something remarkable will happen. Leach gets five wickets and Essex are all out shortly after tea. With only about sixteen overs left in the day, Somerset forfeit their second innings and ask Essex to bat again. Cook apparently averages over 50 on the sub-continent and it shows.

There will be no last-minute collapse. A rather stout-looking Trescothick comes out to field for the last few overs and when the Somerset captain calls time on the match, he leads the players from the field. Essex are the county champions for the second time in three years, and for Somerset, the long wait continues.

When I say goodnight to my son, he admits to becoming annoyed with people on social media questioning Buttler's wicket keeping. He also wants to talk about cricket jumpers, long and sleeveless, which he will need for next season. And new pads. And a new bat...

Later, when I've got the living room to myself, I re-watch the highlights of the World Cup Final – but just from somewhere near the start of England's run chase. Roy is already out and Joe Root - who had been in sublime form and was one of the ICC's top five ranked players for the tournament – is struggling to score a run. The hoardings around the ground proclaim this to be 'The World's Greatest Cricket Celebration' but it doesn't feel like that, even watching it back a couple of months later and knowing the result. There is a queasy unease about England's batting, and the noise in the ground, which is starting to build, feels shrill and nervy.

When he reaches 7 from 28 balls, Root runs down the pitch and has an almighty swish at a ball from Colin de Grandhomme, but misses. The next ball is much wider, and he swishes at it from the crease and does well to get an outside edge and is caught behind.

The wicket is 'dying', according to the Sky commentators, and taking England's batsmen down with it. Bairstow chops on to make it 71-3, and then Morgan is brilliantly caught by Lockie Ferguson running in from deep point. 86-4. The TV cameras pause on a man in the crowd wearing a lion suit, who is standing up with his hands on his head looking disconsolate.

When Buttler joins Stokes, Ian Smith on commentary says 'This is the game' – a bit of a cliché, but it was how it felt in our living room, with my son hopping and up and down, barely able to watch, constantly having to be told to sit down and not walk in front of the TV.

Buttler gets into his stride immediately and seems to be timing the ball, but there are some horrible moments – an edgy drive which doesn't carry to the fielder at third man, and a review for LBW at 142-4. Before that, the fifty partnership between Stokes and Buttler produces another surge of noise in the crowd.

When Buttler steers a wide delivery from Ferguson to the deep point boundary, Sourav Ganguly, the former Indian captain and one of the ICC commentators, makes himself very popular with my son by saying that, 'The ball sounds different off Buttler's bat.' The man in the lion suit is up off his seat and cheering. But the next ball appears to stop in the pitch and Buttler nearly pops it up to cover.

At 182-4 Buttler bails out of an intended ramp shot and delicately sweeps a straight ball to fine leg, and it all seems to be too much for a man in the crowd wearing a white T-shirt, who stands up and gives himself a stiff talking to.

Buttler and Stokes go to their fifties in quick succession but with 46 needed Buttler holes out to the substitute fielder, Tim Southee, at deep point, and the win predictor lurches back in favour of New Zealand.

With 34 needed from 19 balls, the TV cameras spot Prince Andrew - managing to look slightly animated - sitting in the pavilion, surrounded by MCC grandees. Angus Fraser has drawn the short straw of looking after him, but there doesn't appear to be much conversation. The Prime Minister Theresa May, who announced her resignation a week before the tournament started, looks much more excited, and is up on her feet with the rest of her box, craning her neck to see if a Stokes' shot has made it to the boundary.

The next shot of the pavilion at 217-6 shows an empty seat next to an extremely glum-looking Angus Fraser, and HRH nowhere to be seen.

The game is going New Zealand's way and their supporters – many sporting moustaches and sailors' hats – are starting to celebrate. But then Trent Boult carries Stokes' heave to long-on over the boundary and it's down to 16 needed from 8 balls. Archer is bowled first ball, which leaves Stokes to get 15 from the last over.

Dot ball. Dot ball. Six. And then, 'Can you believe this…I do not believe that!' as Stokes accidentally guides Guptill's throw from the deep to the third man boundary. England are not so much having the rub of the green as enjoying a full body massage. Stokes and Buttler sail through the super over, but then there is the awful crack of the ball from Neesham's bat as it flies into the Mound Stand from the second ball of New Zealand's reply. Somehow Archer holds his nerve and bowls fast and straight, and it comes down to two needed from the last ball.

Guptill's clip to midwicket seems to speed up two months on. Roy's pick-up looks even better and the run-out tighter, but the result, thankfully, still hasn't changed.

Losing Monkey

*A short story for
cricket enthusiasts of all ages*

Author's Note

I have decided to call this account of my last holiday Losing Monkey as a sharp reminder to Maya – the ten-year-old girl who owns me – never to lose me again.

From the safety and comfort of her bedroom it is possible to think more calmly about the events which took place in Sri Lanka over the Easter holiday. Although I was naturally upset at the time, Maya has been forgiven. I know she was very upset about everything that occurred and she has apologised profusely since. I am keen to avoid any note of recrimination or bitterness, and have requested that my editor – an extremely wise old ape, who has been tasked with the job of translating my jabbering noises for a wider readership – should remove anything that smacks of sour grapes.

These things happen from time to time to domesticated animals, a price we pay for our lives of luxury and ease, and in my case extensive foreign travel.

Day 1

The story of my disappearance begins in Tissa, close to the southern tip of Sri Lanka. This wasn't the start of the Baxter's holiday, but was the first day that felt to Maya, her brother John, and Mr Baxter, like being on holiday. Mrs Baxter had followed her usual policy of loading the first few days of the holiday with exhausting excursions and sightseeing. I am generally spared the worst of this and am left back at the hotel when the family go out for the day. The room at the Serenity Hotel in Kandy – our first stop – was spacious and air conditioned and I was happy to sit out the dangerous tuk-tuk ride into town and the Temple of the Tooth. Buddhist temples, and place of worship generally, aren't really my cup of tea, and even Mrs Baxter seemed a little unenthusiastic when she arrived back at the hotel hot and fatigued. Mr Baxter's facial expression tends to give even less away on holiday, though he sometimes has a faraway look and, on these occasions, I suspect he'd like to be somewhere else. Maya seemed the most cheerful member of the family on their return and hugged me warmly. Her brother John acknowledged me briefly and then disappeared onto the balcony with his phone. He seems to have undergone profound changes since last year's holiday and has started to behave as if he also wished he was somewhere else. Armed with the hotel's wifi code, he spent the evening on the internet finding out about the poisonous snakes, crocodiles and spiders one is likely to encounter in Sri Lanka, and shooting accusing looks at his parents.

Day 2

The scenic train ride from Kandy through the hilly tea plantations proved to be less relaxing than it sounded when Mrs Baxter was working out the itinerary at the kitchen table at the end of January. Her failure to reserve first class seats had been the cause of some – as it turned out, well-founded – anxiety.

Maya has taken me with her on the train to London on several occasions. When we get on the train at our local railway station it's usually virtually empty, although it fills up by the time we reach Finsbury Park. This wasn't anything like that. As the train pulled in – a fairly short one, consisting of only about four or five carriages – it was obvious that there was barely even room for me, let alone a family of four, each pulling behind them one of those modern style suitcases on wheels. I might have found a space up on one of the luggage racks, but there was no chance of the Baxters getting on. Mr Baxter made a desperate attempt to get in the first- class carriage, but the ticket inspector barked something about 'reservation' and shook his head. A few of the long-haired back packers squeezed into the space at the end of each carriage, but they were travelling rather more lightly than the Baxters.

When the train had gone Mr Baxter said something under his breath I had never heard before and then walked to the end of the platform and kicked a plastic dustbin.

When he re-joined the rest of the family they were talking to an elderly Australian couple, who'd also been left stranded.

Being driven round another bend on the train to Ella

Suddenly everything seemed less miserable. Instead of bemoaning their bad luck like whinging pommes – which is what the Australians sometimes call English people – the couple were cracking jokes and offering to share a taxi if they all got really stuck. In the end this wasn't necessary. A special tourist train was being laid-on, it was announced. Mrs Baxter took a rather theatrical deep breath and exhaled slowly, and Mr Baxter stopped muttering.

I slept for a lot of the seven-hour journey. One tea plantation looks very much like another after a while and so I dozed quietly in the opening of Maya's rucksack. That was until a group of very noisy Australian tourists woke me up at about the five-hour mark. I suspect that they had also lost interest in the rolling hills passing outside because they spent their time taking selfies with their heads sticking out of the train windows.

Even more fascinating was taking pictures of each other's heads sticking out of the windows, whenever the train went around a bend. I must have closed my eyes as a means of blocking them out and then fallen asleep again.

I woke up to find my arms folded over the rail of a bright green tuk-tuk, and that I was having my photo taken with the driver, who, I gather, had just transported Mrs Baxter, Maya and I up into the hills with our luggage – something of a struggle, it seems, for the tiny vehicle. Mr Baxter and John pulled up soon after in a red tuk-tuk.

After inspecting the bathroom and then the view across the

The green tuk-tuk that got us up the hill in Ella

valley, Mrs Baxter began what she called 'very limited unpacking'. We were supposed to be moving on again the following day, at lunchtime, so, as she explained to Mr Baxter, 'There's really no point in unpacking everything, darling.'

By the time she'd finished, there was no view across the valley, just a dense fog of cloud. 'This is good,' said Mr Baxter.

I didn't go down into the town with them later for their evening meal. When they returned, John and Mr Baxter were talking about something called shisha bars and water pipes, and people called hippies they'd seen in Ella – the town we were staying just outside.

The conversation came to an abrupt end when Mr Baxter shouted, 'How should I know John? I've never smoked a

The clouds starting to close in on our hill-top hotel. Five minutes after this picture was taken, we couldn't see the tree.

water pipe.'

After that everything was rather quiet. Maya and I slept with John on a double bed inside a mosquito net, which kept tickling my nose.

Day 3

This morning we all went to visit a tea factory, which meant another hair raising tuk-tuk ride high up into the hills. It's the Sri Lankan New Year and so nothing was actually happening in the factory. Our guide spoke so quickly and strangely that I could hardly understand anything he was saying. This didn't stop a Canadian woman from asking lots of boring questions and a lady from Yorkshire asking about decaffeinated tea. According to our guide it's full of unhealthy additives. After the tour Mr and Mrs Baxter bought small boxes of tea for their relatives.

We got to our next stop, Tissamaharama, or Tissa for short, in the middle of the afternoon. It was much hotter that it had been in the mountains, and everyone complained that the water in the swimming pool was too warm. Even Mrs Baxter, who always takes ages to get in, admitted it wasn't very refreshing. A

A view of Yala National Park

rather long iguano appeared just behind the sun lounger I was sitting on and gave us a bit of a fright. It didn't help that John told everyone that it was a komodo dragon, which I have heard is one of the deadliest predators.

Day 4

A very early start because we all went on safari. I am not an early riser as a rule. In England, on week days, I like to hear the front door shutting in the morning when the Baxters go off to work and the children go to school. I enjoy having the bed to myself and usually doze through the morning.

I wasn't desperate to see a leopard close up, but this didn't seem to occur to anyone else and I was packed in my usual place in the opening of Maya's rucksack. I needn't have worried. The high point for the family was a brief glimpse of a pair of leopards, loping through the brush about two hundred yards away. This caused great excitement and a long tail back of jeeps and an unpleasant fug of diesel fumes.

Unlike wild monkeys, to whom I was made to wave on more than one occasion, I lead a fairly sedentary life and so started to experience motion sickness after a couple of hours of plunging and lurching over the rough track. In total we spent four hours driving round and round the National Park, in the course of which we came across the following: numerous water buffalo, several inert crocodiles, a mongoose, wart hogs, monkeys, and right at the end, a family of elephants. By that time Mr and Mrs Baxter had had enough and instructed the driver to return to the hotel.

It hadn't been one of my better days out with the family. Indirectly, I blame the pair of leopards we saw in the distance for what happened next, and led to me being lost. Maya and her brother spent most of the drive back to the hotel earnestly discussing which big cat they should adopt through the WWF – an Amur leopard, a tiger, or a jaguar. I am not even sure, as Mr

Baxter pointed out, that jaguars are an endangered species, but both children still seemed determined to save them. There was no mention of helping any types of primate, just the terrifying killing machines that make it unsafe to leave the safety of the high branches.

Back at the hotel room I was carelessly tipped out of the rucksack, and slipped off the double bed, onto the floor, out of view. I wasn't unduly concerned because Mrs Baxter is nothing if not thorough, and always likes to conduct a forensic review of the family's luggage before she'll go anywhere.

On this occasion she was less than impressed by the contribution from the rest of her family, who were busy mucking about in the swimming pool, even though their taxi was due any minute. After zipping up each of the large suit cases, she wheeled them out onto the balcony for Mr Baxter and the hotel staff to carry down the stairs. But there was no last-minute checking under the bed, perhaps because she would have had to go down on all fours and do it herself.

The last thing I heard from any of the Baxters was Mrs Baxter shouting, 'Would you please get out of that pool and give me your wet things!'

And then the door closed. Despite the seriousness of my situation, I found myself, as I do at home when I hear the front door shut, dozing off.

About an hour later I was woken up by the wet sponge on the end of a mop, and sent skidding into the dusty floor under the head of the king-sized bed. Two members of the hotel staff were busy preparing the room for the next guests, who arrived

In happier times at the Serenity Hotel in Kandy (day one)

shortly after – Brad and Pattie from Minnesota, in the United States of America. I know this because this is the first thing the man told the other guests when he got chatting to them in the pool or the restaurant, and because he spoke so loudly, I could hear him wherever he went in the hotel.

Mr Baxter doesn't seem to like talking very much and only occasionally raises his voice, but Brad didn't stop talking at the top of his voice for the day and a half that we shared room 502, and to make matters worse, he hardly ever left the room. Most of the time he talked to the TV, which was left on even when they went for dinner in the evenings, or when he joined Pattie briefly by the pool. 'Hey sweetie. You ok?' I would hear him bellow as he clattered down the stairs outside the room. 'I am going to the bar, sweetie. You want me to get you anything.'

On one occasion Patti came back to the room to find Brad standing in front of the TV, staring blankly with a look of total confusion. There was a game of cricket from Galle on the sports channel.

'You ok, honey?'

After a short delay Brad snapped out of his trance and said, 'Hey babe. You gotta see these guys. It's about a hundred degrees out there and these boys are wearing long pants, gloves, crash helmets, and they run in before they pitch it to the batter. It's that crazy game the Brits play in summer. Cricket.'

'Ok honey. You coming out?'

'Might as well,' Brad replied sadly. 'I was looking for a ball game or some hockey, but this is all they got.'

Brad also talked a lot on the telephone to something called room service. 'Hey, can we have some chicken wings for 502. And a couple of beers with that…'

The only time that Brad stopped talking was when he went to sleep, and then he snored – as Pattie said to somebody she was trying to talk to on the phone – like a 'dying wart hog', until she turned him over on his side. Any movements he made as he lay above me produced disconcerting creaks and groans from the frame of the double bed, and the depressing thought that I might be crushed at any minute if it gave way.

Day 5

This brief period of rather uncomfortable cohabitation came to an end on Sunday evening, when Pattie caught sight of me whilst trying to retrieve one of Brad's socks from under the bed, and let out a terrified scream.

'Brad! Brad! Wake up for Christ's sake!'

'What is it, sweetie?'

'There's a monkey under the bed.'

The frame of the bed groaned as he sat up and swung himself up onto his feet. 'Jesus. What do you mean a monkey? What you talking about, babe?'

'See for yourself. I am getting out of here,' she said, wrapping a towel around her.

'No. I am coming with you honey. Hold on,' Brad shouted and slammed the door shut behind him.

A few minutes later they returned with the hotel manager. Brad's familiar voice seemed to have gone up an octave. 'They can be feisty as hell, let me tell you. You don't want to be sleeping with one of them under the bed!'

'If you'd permit me to enter, sir, I think I may be able to put your mind at rest,' the hotel manager said calmly.

'You go right ahead. But we'll be looking for a new hotel, soon as we can get our things.'

The hotel manager came in quietly, knelt down beside the bed, looked at me in a friendly fashion and said, 'Young man, you have been causing everyone a great deal of trouble. I think you had better come with me.'

Back out on the balcony Brad was embracing Pattie, who

had started to cry.

'You were perfectly correct, madam, but there is no need to be alarmed. This monkey belongs to the little girl who was staying in this room before you. Her parents have just contacted me and asked me to look for him. There is really no need to look for a new hotel, I hope you will agree,' the manager said, smiling broadly.

'I guess not,' said Brad flatly. 'Jesus, sweetie, we need to get you to the optometrist. I need a lie down.'

The manager carried me to the reception area and sat me on the hatch between the hotel kitchen and the garden restaurant. A middle-aged man and woman were working hard in the kitchen preparing curries, which they served out in small bowls on trays, like the hot meze they served in the Turkish restaurant I once visited with Maya and her parents.

Every so often the young man on reception would stick his head through the hatch and say, 'Man in 502 again. Two more plates of chicken wings. Extra barbecue sauce.'

My absence, I discovered much later, was only spotted when the Baxters retired for bed the previous evening, having finally arrived at their new hotel. This, I will admit didn't make me feel very good, because I have always regarded myself as much more than a cuddly toy / bed time accessory. Much more pleasing was the family's reaction to my disappearance. Maya went very quiet, apparently frozen by the realisation of her carelessness, and John, I was told, began to cry. Given that most of my previous interaction with Maya's brother has involved him kidnapping me and then demanding a ransom, in the form of chocolate, for my release, this was both surprising and rather gratifying. Mrs Baxter carried out a thorough search of their new room and suit cases, solemnly declared me lost, and immediately sent an email marked 'urgent' to the hotel in Tissa.

Later in the afternoon the hotel manager's two children appeared in the reception area – a girl of about Maya's age, and her brother, who looked a year or two older. Picking me up roughly by one of my ears, the boy swung me in front of his sister's face. 'Is this your new special friend?' he sneered. 'He looks like you!'

If the girl, who had never seen me before, had only told him the truth and denied all knowledge of me, her brother would probably have lost interest and put me back on the hatch. Instead she squealed, 'Give him back!' and started chasing her brother round the garden.

This went on for nearly five minutes. Just as I was starting to feel the onset of motion sickness, the boy stopped at the far end of the garden and sat me on a metal spike. Fortunately, the spike went up into what looked like a tin can, where I was placed next to a long stick, to which were tied several colourful looking cylinders.

'Take another step and monkey goes into orbit,' shouted the boy, brandishing a cigarette lighter in the direction of his sister. 'Another move and no New Year for monkey. Go on. Get lost!'

But before I had a chance to fully appreciate the danger I was in, the hotel manager appeared, as if by magic, bounding towards us down the garden. 'Give me that cigarette lighter this instant! What are you doing you silly boy? This monkey is the property of one of our customers and I have promised to return it to them, in one piece. So do not attach it to a rocket. I will put a rocket up your backside if I see you playing with fireworks again. Take the monkey out of there and follow me,' he said to his daughter. 'I have promised to post this monkey to the little girl's hotel in Mirissa. We cannot afford another misadventure. Please pack him in a secure parcel ready for posting tomorrow.'

The girl followed her father to an office room behind the hotel reception. 'Everything you need is here. Make sure you wrap him up securely,' he said. 'And when you have finished put him in this box with the other post.'

The girl cut a square sheet from a roll of bubble wrap and laid it on the table. I had seen bubble wrap before – Mrs Baxter uses it when she is selling things on ebay – but it hadn't occurred to me it might be used for a soft toy like me, and Sri Lanka isn't the climate in which I'd have chosen to be wrapped up in clammy plastic. For a moment I lay on my back with the sensation of being on a transparent air bed. Had I been allowed to remain in this position I would almost certainly have dozed off. Instead I found myself being turned round and round, behind an ever thickening layer of plastic bubbles. I found this extremely disorientating. Apart from the obvious sensation of claustrophobia and muffled sound, the bubbles projected a very odd view of the outside world and gave everything bulging curves. When I looked up at the little girl doing this to me, she peered back through enormous frog-like eyes beneath a bulbous forehead.

That was the last thing I remember seeing. Then I must have passed out. When I came to, the bubble wrap had gone and the manager was talking sternly to his daughter. 'What are you doing you silly girl? This stuff is for fragile or valuable objects –

not a well-padded monkey, who I am sure doesn't want to be suffocated before he goes home. What have I told you about putting your head in plastic bags? What are you trying to do to him! We will find some thick brown paper.'

'What are *you* doing with that monkey, you silly man?' demanded a voice I didn't recognise. A lady dressed in a colourful sari appeared in the doorway. 'Your uncle and his family are arriving in twenty minutes. The family in twenty-two from Yorkshire are making a fuss about their bill, and what is my husband doing? Playing pass-the-parcel with a toy monkey!' She folded her arms and sent a withering look in the direction of her husband. 'Can you talk to Mr Bathgate, please. I can't understand anything he says.'

The manager picked me up, hurried out to reception and sat me on the front desk next to an old portable television. A thick set man was peering over the top of his glasses, studying a thin strip of paper. Next to him a small lady was tapping away on her phone. It was the woman from the tea factory who'd asked about decaffeinated tea. 'No. You divide it by six, love,' she was saying.

'Are you alright?' the man said to the manager.

'Good evening, Mr Bathgate. Can I help?' said the manager smiling.

'It's our bill. Reckon it might be more than it should be,' the man said grimly. 'Could you do us a print out, with everything listed. What do you call those things?'

'An itemised bill,' his wife said eagerly.

'That's it. An itemised bill. Could you let us have one of those please?'

'Yes of course Mr Bathgate. Is there anything else I can help you with?'

'No, you're alright.'

'How was the safari this morning?' added the manager.

'It were alright, weren't it love. But it were a lot of driving. Saw a lot of water buffalo, some flamingo. But didn't see any leopards or elephants. And that wasn't cheap, neither.'

The manager smiled and went back into the office.

'Oh, look Pete. Do you think Alice would like to play with that monkey?' said the lady. 'Just until the taxi gets here – because I've packed all her toys.'

'Might as well. Only monkey I've seen since we got here.' He reached over the desk and picked me up in his big rubbery hands, before handing me to a little girl doing some colouring in at one of the tables. 'She can do a flippin' makeover on him,' the man muttered under his breath.

The girl, it turned out, wasn't using colouring pens but was trying out a selection of lip sticks and eye liners on a piece of paper. 'Can I do his make-up, mummy?' the girl asked.

'I shouldn't think anyone'd mind. But make sure you don't get it on your clothes. There's nothing else you can wear. It's all packed,' the woman said wearily.

For the next two hours my eyes and lips were coated in every colour combination the little girl could think of. Heat and a thick coating of make-up do not go well together and did nothing for my spirits, which were already extremely low.

At one point her younger brother insisted on having a go with the lipstick, and was even less of an expert than his sister. The small mirror set up on the table in front of me showed what looked like an angry red scar running from my mouth under my chin.

Eventually their mother reappeared and shouted, 'Kids! Taxi's here. Come on. Time to go.' And then after a moment's pause, 'Can you both have a wee please.'

I watched the little girl putting her make-up away in her glittery pencil case, and felt a surge of relief run through me. No matter that she'd left me with brilliant green lips, the remains of a huge scar, and boggly yellow eyes. At least I might finally be able to get some sleep after a long and eventful day.

This thought proved to be a bit premature. First of all, I was witness to a rather heated conversation between the manager and his wife.

'You shouldn't have backed down. The man (I presume they were talking about Mr Bathgate) was impossible,' the manager's wife said from behind the reception desk.

'That is precisely why I couldn't be bothered to argue, my dear. Seven English pence is all it cost us to quieten him down and send him on his way happy.'

'But it is the principle of the thing!' returned his wife. 'You should never give in to bullies.'

The manager smiled. 'I am not sure I would call Mr Bathgate a bully. He was really much too silly to be a bully. Every time he added up the items on the bill he arrived at a different figure. On the last count he said that we'd overcharged them by seven pence. I couldn't face watching him add it all up again for the sake of seven pence. His daughter, however, has been bullying our friend monkey. Look what she's done to him. He looks ridiculous.' The manager took me back to the reception desk to show his wife. 'Do you think we could put him in the washing machine?'

'Don't be silly!' his wife replied. 'Men know nothing about fabric. Look at his bottom, how threadbare it looks. We can't risk putting him in the washing machine.'

I wasn't happy about her use of the word 'threadbare' but I was grateful that she'd saved me from the washing machine, which, I know from previous experience, is no picnic. One weekend about a year ago, Mrs Baxter put me in her washing machine with what she called a mixed load. It could have been even worse, apparently. There are hotter washes and longer cycles, which would have been even more uncomfortable, but it was bad enough – like being whizzed round in a food blender, just without the blades. Mrs Baxter was all for putting me in the tumble dryer after the wash, but fortunately Maya rescued me and let me dry out gently on her window sill.

'So can I leave it to you, dear?' said the manager.

'He needs to soak in a hot tub,' she said picking me up and heading towards the kitchen.

The hot tub turned out to be a plastic washing up bowl, and two inches of warm, soapy water.

This would have been the ideal moment for a nap, but just as I closed my eyes, there was a succession of loud explosions from the garden beyond the swimming pool. The fireworks had started.

They continued with varying degrees of intensity for the next half hour. When it stopped the, manager's wife re-appeared and set about my make-up with some sort of brillo pad. I had been fearing a good hard scrubbing, but, true to her word, she was extremely gentle. In fact, it was rather ticklish, and I had to try not to laugh.

Day 6

That was my last recollection of an extremely eventful day. I woke up the next morning in the basket of a bicycle, parked next to the outside dining area. The manager and his family, and also his brother's family, were eating breakfast. The manager's wife was taking him to task on my account. 'Mrs Baxter said that they are leaving on Friday. How do you think the monkey will get there by post before then? Brother, talk some sense into him, would you. And pass the water melon please.'

The manager did as he was told and turned to look at the man sitting at the end of the table, who looked like an older version of him.

'My sister is right,' he said. 'You should always listen to your wife, brother. About this sort of thing women always know best. You know, I am still waiting for the headphones I ordered last month. I wouldn't send anything of value by post.' Then after a short pause the man added, 'I think we can help you brother. Marvin and Kumara have got nothing to do this week,' he said looking at the two young men to his right. 'Boys, you can help your uncle and take this monkey to Mirissa for him.'

He didn't appear to require an answer. Both boys looked up from their breakfast and nodded dutifully.

'Then that is settled. You can set off when you have finished eating.'

Later, when the manager and his wife were clearing away the breakfast things, she said, 'Is this wise asking Marvin and Kumara to help? I know you are very fond of your nephews, but Marvin would forget his head if it wasn't screwed on. Supposing he loses Monkey somewhere on the way. How will we explain that to Mrs Baxter? And I am surprised your brother lets him ride around on that moped considering what he is like.'

'I know he's a bit dopey, but he's a good boy and Kumara is sensible. He will look after Monkey and his elder brother. And I don't think we have any choice,' he said shrugging his shoulders.

Given what I'd overheard, I was relieved to find I'd be travelling in the jacket pocket of the younger brother. Unfortunately, Marvin was driving the tiny moped. The manager gave Kumara the address of the Baxters' hotel and some money to buy some food on the journey. Then he turned to me and said, 'Goodbye Monkey. I hope you have enjoyed your stay with us. Have a safe journey.'

Had we been in a busy town, I suspect travelling on Marvin's moped would have been even more terrifying than the tuk-tuk ride from the Serenity Hotel in Kandy. His driving didn't inspire confidence. Our first near-collision came after only ten minutes when we almost drove straight into a herd of buffalo being led across the road by a farmer. From then on Kumara kept up a stream of reminders and instructions. When we passed a succession of families bathing in the river beside the road, Marvin waved and shouted something I couldn't understand.

'Can you keep your hands on the bike! You're all over the place!' shouted Kumara. 'Have you seen that bus coming towards us?'

'Of course I can see the bus!' Marvin shouted over his shoulder. 'Can you stop complaining little brother. Just try and relax.'

'Easy to say,' sighed Kumara, and squeezed his jacket pocket to check I was still there.

Only the top of my head was sticking out from his pocket. In Sri Lanka they drive on the left like in England, so for most of the journey I had a view of the sea, and the fishermen perched high up on stilts. Mrs Baxter had spoken at some length to Maya and John about this traditional method of fishing on the flight, though I suspect I may have been paying closer attention than them.

It was extremely cosy in Kumara's pocket. The warm sea air and drone of the moped were a strangely soothing combination and I quickly forgot all about Marvin's driving and dozed off.

It's never a good idea to sleep for too long in the day, and I woke up feeling unusually disorientated. I was still, I realised, in Kumara's pocket, but we weren't on the moped. That appeared

A fisherman's perch

to be parked some way off in the shade of an enormous tree. I, on the other hand, seemed to have woken up in the middle of a game of cricket. Kumara was standing sideways on, with his knees slightly bent, looking down a strip of bare matting. A stocky figure with a mop of curly hair was charging towards us. When he reached the stumps at the other end of the wicket, he launched something at us that flew past Kumara's nose into the hands of another boy standing behind the stumps at our end. He then rolled it back up the matting to the bowler and I could see that it was a black rubber ball. Kumara wasn't wearing any of the protective equipment I'd seen Maya's brother wear on one occasion in the back garden. Not that any of that would have helped me inside Kumara's jacket pocket, so it was a relief to see that they weren't playing with a real ball. But even a tennis ball would hurt if it were propelled quickly enough – and this looked much harder and more threatening than a tennis ball, and was being sent down at serious speed.

The next ball landed closer to us and Kumara lunged forward with his bat, but missed.

'You've got junior fishing! Reel him in big man,' shouted the boy behind the wickets.

'Put some pepper on it!' shouted one of the other fielders, which also seemed an odd thing to say in a cricket match, but I suspected it wasn't good news for Kumara, or myself, and so it proved. The next ball arrowed into Kumara's body even more quickly and whistled past his hip, and over my head sticking out of his pocket.

'Come on little brother. Show me the face of the bat, will you. This is getting boring,' snarled the bowler.

I didn't see the next delivery because I sank down further into Kumara's pocket, but I felt the vibration when it hit the bat.

'Don't let him do that to you!' shouted one of the fielders. 'Send him home, big man.'

I made myself watch the next ball, which Kumara managed to nudge round the corner to where Marvin was fielding.

'Run junior!' shouted the batsman at the other end, and suddenly we were sprinting towards the scary bowler. Kumara needn't have bothered because his brother barely reacted, and appeared to be daydreaming.

'Marvin! Wake up man! What was that?' demanded the bowler. 'You trying to help little brother get off the mark? Keep up, will you boy.'

Marvin mumbled an apology and made an attempt to look like he was on his toes for the next delivery.

Kumara tried to hit the next bowler – a much slower bowler

– into the tree where the moped was parked. Unfortunately, his enormous swipe didn't connect with the ball, and he was stumped by the wicket keeper, who celebrated noisily. 'That's how you do it, Marvin! Watch and learn, sleepy head.'

I was secretly relieved that Kumara's innings was over, and now that the immediate danger had passed, my thoughts turned to the other pressing matter of my reunion with the Baxters, although this seemed to be the last thing on anyone's mind. Marvin was wandering around the outfield, seemingly in a world of his own, whilst Kumara had now taken over behind the stumps and was trying to distract the new batsman. 'This monkey hits the ball harder than you. Everyone come in five paces. He won't hit it off the square.'

I wasn't sure how to react to this, but, as it turned out, Kumara was right. I might have done a better job. After missing his first three deliveries, the next ball was pitched shorter. The batsman stepped back to take evasive action, and fell backwards over the stumps, to the amusement of the bowler and all of the fielders.

At the end of the next over, Kumara removed his jacket, in which I was being transported, and wandered over to where the moped was parked in the shade. He hung it neatly from the handlebars, from where I could continue to watch the game. It was very pleasant in the shade and the jacket swung gently in the sea breeze. Had it not been for the incessant chattering of the monkeys in the tree above me I might have nodded off. I had to admire their energy levels. Some of the smaller monkeys seemed to be in perpetual motion, and provided rather more action for the spectator than the game of cricket.

Marvin, who was fielding in the outfield in front of me,

hardly moved at all. Every now and then the bowler or one of the other fielders would shout something in his direction and he would start walking in, but it would only be for a couple of deliveries.

After one of the deliveries when he wasn't walking in as the bowler ran in to bowl there was a loud chorus of 'catch it'. Marvin looked up and started walking round in little circles as he tried to position himself for the catch.

'You've got him Marvin!' shouted one of the fielders encouragingly.

'Turn your hands up and stand still!' shouted the bowler with a note of desperation.

When the ball finally came down, it bounced off Marvin's shoulder and thudded into the wheel of the moped next to me.

'That's a six!' shouted the batsmen at the bowler's end.

'That's a joke!' shouted the bowler bitterly. 'Go and sit down please, Marvin. I'd rather have no one at square leg!'

The other fielders seemed to find this very funny. Marvin did what he was told and slumped down in the shade next to me. From his rucksack he took out the food his aunt had given them, which was wrapped in silver foil.

I like silver foil because it scares the Baxters' cat, who I am wary of to the say the least. He's never shown any interest in me, or in any of Maya's soft toys, but I have sometimes heard Mr and Mrs Baxter complain about a dead mouse or rabbit they have found on the patio in the morning, and I know what he's capable of. But whenever Mrs Baxter unrolls the silver foil he seems to panic and runs for his life.

Marvin arranged the food around him – some flat bread, an assortment of brown savoury snacks (probably bhajis and pakoras) and slices of watermelon.

'I was joking, you clown!' shouted the bowler.

Everyone also seemed to find this very funny as well.

Marvin scrambled to his feet and hurried back on to the outfield to re-join the game.

As soon as he had taken up his position, I heard a rustle in the tree and then the soft thud of several monkeys hopping down from the lower branches, eager to share Marvin's packed lunch. In fact, it was supposed to be Marvin and Kumara's lunch, and none of the monkeys seemed very keen on sharing.

When they had polished off all of the food, they searched inside the rucksack for anything else they could eat, and then, when that produced nothing, began to poke around inside Kumara's jacket.

Just as the largest of the three monkeys came face to face with me in the side pocket, they were startled by a furious cry of 'Marvin!' from Kumara. And then, 'Behind you!'

I don't know if the note of urgency in Kumara's voice was out of consideration for me, and the danger I might be in, or because one of the monkeys was looking in his inside pocket – the one where men tend to keep their wallet – or simply because he'd realised they'd eaten all his lunch. Perhaps it was a combination of all three that made him sound so angry and panicked the monkey into grabbing me before he scooted back up into the tree.

Marvin finally burst into life and sprinted back to where he'd left his lunch just a couple of minutes earlier. His brother and some of the other fielders arrived shortly after.

'I must be dreaming,' Kumara said witheringly. 'Tell me you haven't just left our lunch lying about under a tree full of hungry monkeys?'

Marvin shuffled unhappily from foot to foot and nodded his head.

'Nice one Sherlock!' said one of the other boys.

'And there's a more serious problem,' Kumara said gravely. 'They've got Monkey.'

'What are you talking about?' asked the other boy, pulling a face. 'Do you two have your own code or something?'

'The toy monkey that was in my pocket, you idiot,' replied Kumara sharply. 'We're supposed to be taking him to Mirissa for my uncle.'

By this point I was directly above the circle of boys. Their voices carried up into the middle part of the tree where I was sat with my captor. Rather, he was sat, and I was tucked under his arm so that he had both of his hands free for scratching his head and upper body. This was preferable to being held in his mouth, which had been the case for four or five dizzying seconds as he shot up into the tree. Real monkey dribble and teeth came as a nasty shock.

Eventually I plucked up the courage to look down from what, to me, felt like our extremely precarious perch. The game of cricket had come to a complete halt and the pieces of equipment – the bat and ball, and the stumps – were now being readied, it appeared, for something else. The fast bowler with the mop of curly hair had the ball and appeared to be taking aim in our direction. The ball whistled over the head of the monkey holding me and bounced violently against the branches above us, before dropping back to earth. The monkey didn't hang around for the next attempt but clambered further up into the tree and hid himself behind the leaves.

The next flying object to be launched in our direction was a cricket stump. Fortunately, this hit one of the lower branches and crashed back down onto the head of the boy who'd thrown it, much to the amusement of everyone else.

More stumps followed and also the bat, in a scene which reminded me of an occasion when I'd watched John and Maya throwing sticks into a conker tree. It was gratifying that they were taking some trouble to rescue me, but I had mixed feelings about the hard rubber ball – the only projectile which got further than the lower branches – and the intentions of the boy with the curly hair.

Fortunately, it isn't cool to spend too much time and effort on behalf of a soft toy when you are in your late teens, and fairly quickly the other boys lost interest and went their own ways. Marvin and Kumara gave up trying to knock me and the real monkey from our perch, and sat down next to the moped. Kumara produced a packet of chewing gum from his pocket and offered a piece to his brother.

'Some supper, brother?' he said cheerfully.

'I am sorry,' Marvin sighed miserably. 'I shouldn't have left the food out.'

'No.'

'Or dropped that catch.'

'No.'

'What are we going to do?'

Kumara shrugged his shoulders and then lay down on his back with an attitude of resignation.

The sun was beginning to drop down onto the sea in the distance. Now that they were no longer being bombarded from below, the six or seven monkeys in the tree started up a noisy chatter.

Kumara rolled on to his side and propped himself up on his elbow. 'What was in auntie's packed lunch? I might as well know.'

'Can we not talk about it please.'

'Flatbread?'

'Yes.'

'Bhajis?'

'Yes.'

'Desert?'

'Yes.'

'What?'

'Water melon.'

'Anything else?'

'Two pakoras each.'

Kumara rubbed his face and groaned. 'Perhaps the question should be what are *you* going to do?' he said, fixing his eyes on his brother. 'You have got us into this pickle. Any ideas how to get us out of it?'

Marvin looked as if he were trying to speak but ended up saying nothing.

Kumara said, 'These people are leaving tomorrow afternoon. Father will go mad if we don't deliver this monkey to Mirissa. The girl's parents will probably leave a nasty review on Trip Advisor saying how unhelpful auntie and uncle have been. We'll never hear the last of it.'

I shared the boys' deepening sense of gloom. The fact that it was getting dark didn't help and there didn't appear to be any immediate prospect of a reversal of fortune.

* * *

There would shortly be a reversal of sorts, but it didn't really help the situation.

The monkey, who had had me tucked under his arm, lost interest in me not long after the cricket players, and let me drop onto a tangle of leaves and flimsy branches. One of the problems of having no spine is that I can't sit up without assistance. This meant that when I landed on my back I had to stay in that position and had no idea just how precarious my position was. Every time there was any breeze, I felt the tangle of branches sway. Any stronger gust of wind, I concluded, would probably untangle them and send me crashing to earth.

After a few minutes in this uncomfortable position, that is exactly what happened. One of the advantages of being a soft toy is that I have plenty of padding and so enjoyed a soft landing. Had I made a bit more noise the boys might have noticed my return, but because I came to ground on the other side of the tree it went undetected.

The real monkeys in the tree, whose hearing is much more acute, did notice my fall and it set them off chattering at top volume. Kumara and Marvin weren't to know that they were overreacting and jumped to the understandable conclusion that there must be some sort of dangerous predator – perhaps a leopard – close by. Kumara jumped up and wheeled the moped so that it was leaning against the tree trunk, and then hopped on to the seat and pulled himself up into the tree from one of the lower branches. Marvin followed his example with far more dexterity than he'd shown on the cricket field, and both boys settled on a large branch near to the middle of the tree. Their presence provoked even more noise from the monkeys above and persuaded the boys that the danger / leopard must be real, and from then on, they communicated in a low whisper, which I could hardly hear from the ground.

This is how things happened with the benefit of hindsight. At the time I wasn't to know that there was no leopard. I'd already had a brief encounter with the inside of a monkey's mouth, and was aware that that would probably feel like child's play compared to the jaws of a leopard.

Presently it quietened down, and in the quiet there was a definite low growl.

Marvin jumped to his feet and began pulling himself further up the tree.

'Get down, you idiot!' hissed Kumara. 'That was my stomach rumbling. Do you think those monkeys would have shut up if there was leopard out there.'

'No, I suppose not,' said Marvin returning to the lower branches.

That was quite reassuring, and, unlike the two boys, who spent the next few hours fighting off sleep in order not to fall out of the tree, I allowed myself to shut my eyes and, fairly quickly, dozed off. Their only topic of conversation I can recall, before I lost consciousness, was what they'd eat when they got to Mirissa, and how much they could get with the money their uncle had given them.

When I woke up, not for the first time on this holiday, it took me a few moments to work out what was going on. My back was all wet, probably from the early morning dew, but much more disorientating, was that I seemed to be flying. Kumara, who had presumably just discovered me lying under the tree in the half light of the early morning, was celebrating as if he had just taken a catch – by hurling me up into the sky, whilst he performed a dance of celebration as he waited for me to come down. When Marvin cottoned on, he joined in the strange dance, and the two boys threw me back and forth between them for a bit.

'Come on. We should be going,' said Kumara, and, very gently, pushed me back down into his jacket pocket.

They gathered up the pieces of silver foil and plastic drinks bottles and stuffed them in the rucksack. The moped started first time, and we trundled across the dusty field towards the main road.

For half an hour or so we had the coast road virtually to ourselves. Gradually, as the day started, traffic started to build up, and there were more potential hazards for Kumara to worry about. 'Watch that truck in front of us, Marvin! He hasn't seen us so keep your distance. And slow down!'

Neither of them was wearing a crash helmet. It was hard not to think about the Baxters' new car, which bleeped with increasing intensity every second that somebody's seat belt wasn't fastened, and sometimes caused Mr Baxter to curse modern technology.

We reached Mirissa by the middle of the morning. Kumara, who was looking at a map on his phone, provided directions to the hotel, which was situated in a quiet back street close to the beach. They parked the moped outside a side door and passed through into a shaded courtyard, where there was a swimming pool and a bar area. Two men were clearing away the breakfast things and another was scooping leaves out of the pool with a net.

'Excuse me,' said Kumara clearing his throat, 'we are looking for Mr and Mrs Baxter.'

'They're not here. I saw them go twenty minutes ago,' said one of the men without looking up, and he carried on wiping a table.

This meant that he didn't see Kumara and Marvin sink to their haunches with their heads in their hands, in an attitude of obvious despair.

'You ok boys? They'll be back in a bit,' the man added when he looked up from the table and saw their faces. 'They've just gone to the beach.'

The man gave them directions to somewhere called the Secret Beach, which he said was a short drive up a steep track.

The little moped struggled gamely up the winding road up out of Mirissa, and then turned a tight bend and plunged down an even steeper and rougher section of road towards the sea.

The name 'Secret Beach' struck me as rather misleading. It was tucked away in an extremely secluded spot, but lots of people seemed to know about it. There was also loud reggae music playing from an enormous speaker in the snack bar, still in the process of being built beneath the trees behind the beach. The owner of the bar said something to Marvin and Kumara, which looked to me like half greeting and half challenge – as in 'What are you two boys doing here?'

When Kumara explained who they were looking for the man pulled a face and motioned them to follow him.

On the beach the music was being drowned out by a different kind of wailing. A group of people were standing around a sun lounger where the noise was coming from.

'Take it easy, will you, big man,' said the barman to the source of the crying. 'You'll scare away the customers. Somebody here to see you.'

The crowd parted to reveal John lying on his front, with his right foot in the air, and Mrs Baxter in close attendance with a pair of tweezers.

'Try to keep still, John,' she was saying, her patience clearly frayed.

'Our man has had a little accident with the coral. Very painful I should think. Can I get you a drink boy?'

'Can I have a coke please,' snivelled John.

'Coming right up. Your mum's doing her best, so keep the noise down, man. Anyway, these boys want a word with your mum and dad,' he said indicating Marvin and Kumara.

I could see Maya, sat slightly apart on the end of a sun bed, looking rather sadly out to sea. During the post mortem of John's accident later that day, I learnt that she'd been trying to

cheer him up but had been told to, 'Go away and leave me alone!' As soon as Kumara said the words 'Hotel in Tissa', she turned around and, seeing me, shouted, 'Yes! You've got Monkey!'

John jerked his head up from the sun bed and said, 'What?' and then started crying when he saw me being handed to his sister. And then I disappeared from view for what seemed like nearly a minute, as Maya gave me the most enormous hug.

'You're as bad as your brother, girl!' said the barman returning with John's coke. 'I said keep the noise down.'

'You'll have to excuse us,' said Mr Baxter. 'We've just had some very good news. This calls for a celebration.'

'Excuse me sir,' Kumara said, 'my uncle at the hotel in Tissa would like to speak to you,' and handed his mobile phone to Mr Baxter.

'Hello…'

But Mr Baxter's conversation was obliterated by exclamations of 'Monkey!' from John and Maya, their earlier disagreement now forgotten. John was allowed to hold me whilst the last shards of coral were removed from his foot by Mrs Baxter, and even handed me back sensibly when his operation was over.

Mr and Mrs Baxter shook hands rather seriously with Marvin and Kumara, and insisted on paying for their lunch at the snack bar.

Later when the family started getting ready to go back to the hotel, John said, 'Have you got Monkey?'

And a few minutes later, as they started walking up the steep track back to Mirissa, Mr and Mrs Baxter both said, 'Have you got Monkey?'

'Yes!' said Maya warmly, and smiled at me in the opening of her rucksack, which she'd switched round and was wearing

in front of her like a papoose.

While Mr and Mrs Baxter finished packing, Maya and John gave me an exhaustive tour of their hotel. They weren't allowed in the pool, Mrs Baxter decided, because that had led, indirectly, to losing me just before they left the previous hotel in Tissa. Instead I was made to pose for a series of photographs, some of which I have included here.

When the taxi arrived, Maya put me in my usual place in her rucksack, and, because she'd had so many reminders about not leaving me behind, took the unusual extra precaution of zipping it up. For two minutes I was plunged into complete darkness. I could hear Mrs Baxter saying to John, 'Are you sure you checked under your bed?' and then whispering to Mr Baxter, 'Do you think we should leave a tip?' But as soon as she was settled in the back of the taxi, Maya unzipped her rucksack and sat me on her lap for the duration of the long drive to the airport.

Eight days earlier the taxi from Colombo Airport to Kandy had seemed to take for ever. Occasionally there had been bursts of speed as our minibus zig-zagged in and out of people on mopeds, but in the towns the journey had consisted of lurching movements as our driver crawled and fought his way through heavy traffic. This time, at Mr Baxter's insistence, we took the two-lane motorway, and got to the airport in under two hours. Mr Baxter mentioned the quality of the road surface and absence of traffic several times in the course of the drive, and generally appeared more cheerful than usual. Otherwise there was virtually no conversation, the excitement at my return

seemingly displaced by thoughts of the eleven-hour flight home and the return to work and school on Monday. At one point, John took his head phones out and tried to persuade his parents that they could upgrade to business class for the return flight for only £20 extra each. Mr and Mrs Baxter exchanged raised eyebrows but said nothing. Maya, who took what her brother said more seriously, pointed out that if it only cost £20, everyone would do it.

'That's well out of order!' grumbled John – one of his new expressions – and went back to looking at his phone.

Maya and I were separated again, briefly, at airport security. I was placed in a plastic tray next to her training shoes and rucksack, and ducked down as it disappeared along the conveyor belt beneath heavy plastic flaps. For an eerie moment it was pitch black and everything went very quiet.

When I came out on the other side, Mrs Baxter was being patted and pressed by a female customs officer, having set off the security scanner.

A few moments later, when the family were putting on their shoes and collecting their things, the security scanner beeped sharply and a familiar voice groaned, 'You gotta be kidding. Honey, I won't be a second.'

'Ok sweetie. Don't sweat it.'

It was Brad and Patti from the hotel in Tissa. Patti spotted me in the plastic tray and shrieked, 'Brad! Oh my God! You're kidding me!'

'Keep it down for Christ sakes!' boomed Brad, standing to attention with his arms out for the security guard. 'What is it honey?'

'It's that monkey from the hotel!' Patti reached over, picked me out of the tray and waved me at Brad, who was still being frisked by the security man.

'What are you doing?' said Maya fiercely, and snatched me out of Patti's hand.

Patti stepped back, startled. 'I am so sorry sweetheart. That must 'a looked kind of weird.'

Mrs Baxter stepped forward and said, 'I am ever so sorry. That was very rude Maya. Can you apologise please!'

But before Maya had a chance to speak Brad appeared at her shoulder and said, 'Hey little fella. We gotta stop meeting like this,' and then launched into a very long account of our previous encounter.

Mr and Mrs Baxter listened politely, although I noticed Mr Baxter catching Maya's eye at one point and her trying not to laugh.

When Brad had finished, he and Patti asked if they could take a selfie with me, and then attempted to fist bump Maya and her brother before wandering off towards the duty free.

Brad's voice – 'Look sweetie, they've got Jonny Walker half price…' – carried after the Baxters as they looked for somewhere to have a cup of tea and a snack.

As we were boarding the plane two hours later, John's claim about the £20 upgrade came back to me as the Baxters were shuffling slowly down the aisle towards their seats in economy. The stewards were serving the passengers in business class champagne, and some were already stretched out under blankets, looking forward to a comfortable night's sleep. When John and Mr Baxter, who are both tall, took their seats their knees were squashed against the seats in front of them, and when the person in front of John reclined their seat he started complaining theatrically – 'Oh what! I told you we should have done an upgrade.'

He was interrupted by the Chief Steward introducing herself and her team. After she had reminded passengers to close the overhead lockers, and to fasten seat belts and keep seats in an upright position, she added, 'A special welcome to Maya and Monkey, who are travelling back to the UK with Maya's brother John and their parents. To celebrate Monkey's safe return the Captain would like to invite Maya and John and Monkey to visit the cockpit before we prepare for take-off.'

One of the stewards led us to the front of the plane accompanied by rapturous applause started by Mr Baxter. The Captain and First Officer were both Dutch but spoke excellent English and asked Maya lots of questions about her holiday, and also some relating to my disappearance. I was allowed to touch some of the controls and the Captain shook my hand when we left.

'That was well embarrassing,' John said under his breath to Mr and Mrs Baxter when we returned to our seats.

Maya and I had the window seat. It was dark by the time we took off, and the last thing I can recall before I dozed off in her lap, were the lights of Colombo below.

Other books by Adam Tangent

Those Who Can't: A Teacher's Gap Years

Those Who Can't... records a teacher's sticky moments in and out of the classroom - their painful first steps, home and then abroad, as the reluctant teacher tries to avoid lesson planning and the school bell behind the Iron Curtain.

Ambassadors and Zombies: A Teacher's Guide To Schools and Teaching

Who are Ambassadors and Champions? Is there life after Levels? When did the Govian chicken come home to roost? Do you have a growth mindset or are you baffled? *Ambassadors and Zombies* has the answers to those questions and more on what can make you laugh and cry in an English secondary school.

Author Adam Tangent brings experience and authenticity to an unflinching but often humorous account of working in a 21st-century secondary modern school…

Printed in Great Britain
by Amazon